CONCILIUM

concilium   1991/6

THE SPECIAL NATURE OF WOMEN?

Edited by

Anne Carr and
Elisabeth Schüssler Fiorenza

SCM Press · London
Trinity Press International · Philadelphia

December 1991

ISBN: 0 334 03011 0
ISSN: 0010–5236

Typeset at The Spartan Press Ltd, Lymington, Hants
Printed by Mackays of Chatham, Kent

Concilium: Published February, April, June, August, October, December.

Contents

Editorial

The question of women's essential difference is again a focal point of discussion. The assertion that women possess a special nature has been made by a variety of thinkers whose work has been used, directly or indirectly, by Christian theology and practice. Some have used the notion of women's essential nature to confirm traditional and stereotyped understandings of women's limited 'place and role' in society and church. Others have suggested that because of their special nature women have a distinctive and important contribution to make: since women's difference has heretofore been marginalized or suppressed, the unique contributions of women need to be discovered and recognized. This number of *Concilium* seeks to situate the elements of the debate about the nature of women and explore some of its political, social and ecclesial dimensions.

Our first section examines some of the specific struggles in which the issue of 'women's difference' was and is central. The opening article by Ina Praetorius explores the development of the concept of equal rights in the cultural context of the European Enlightenment as it came to include the notion of women's special privileges. She shows how the middle-class ideal of women's nature and women's special function within the family is enmeshed in the discriminations of racism, classism, antisemitism and Eurocentrism, and she offers a vision for the future which takes account of the disastrous consequences of past asymmetry in the understanding of sexual difference.

Rosemary Radford Ruether probes the theme with specific reference to women's struggle for equal rights in the Christian churches, especially with regard to women's participation in leadership, ministry or ordination. She points out that the nature of the being of God and of the human have traditionally been cast in generically male terms in such a way as to subordinate women in both society and church and to exclude women from public leadership in either realm. With the recent access of women to higher education and theological study, women have been able to challenge the patterns of male dominance in social and ecclesial contexts. The more liberal Protestant churches have accepted the feminist critique of the Christian theological tradition and admitted women to ministry, but the

Roman Catholic Church has not. Radford Ruether uses the case of the United States' bishops proposed pastoral letter on the concerns of women to show the conflict between an anthropology of equivalence and partnership and the anthropology of complementarity, the 'biblical anthropology' favoured by Rome. This anthropology, which divides males and females into 'two opposite psycho-symbolic ontologies', has been used by Pope John Paul II to argue for the essential difference between the roles of men and women, especially in the church. This affirmation of essential difference is in contradiction to the assertion of equality in creation and in Christ and indicates a deep incoherence in Catholic theology.

In a third case study of struggle, Kwok Pui-lan analyses the ambiguous situation of the role and function of the 'white lady' in Western colonialism and Christian mission. By exploring the relationship of gender and race in the missionary settings of the nineteenth century, she shows how mission ideology stressed the essential difference between white women and women of colour and how, in some situations, the introduction of Christianity entailed a decrease in participation and freedom for colonized women. The image of the 'white lady' was part of the myth of ethnocentric Western domination over other peoples, who were portrayed as 'the other', while Christian civilization was identified with white culture. Thus Third World women see their own liberation as including liberation from colonialism, economic control and militarism, and understand superimposed, mutually irreconcilable essences as part of the fabric of domination. At the same time, they insist on the uniqueness and difference of people who have been shaped by particular historical and cultural forces.

In a final analysis of particular struggle, Mary John Mananzan uses her own experiences with women in the Philippines to discuss the difference between education to traditional 'femininity' and education to an empowering feminism. While in the past, education in family, church and school participated in a 'gender regime' which inculcated sterotyped constructs of 'masculinity' and 'femininity', the emergence of feminist thought in the 1960s meant a new form of education characterized by cooperative and collaborative methods in which the shared experience of women became collective insights leading to new knowledge. Feminist education today is interdisciplinary, involves women of all classes, races and religions and, in addition to rational approaches, makes use of all the arts in its work toward the emancipation of women.

In our second section, the articles take a historical perspective on the way women's difference has been constructed in the past. Linda Maloney examines the discussion of women (and slaves) in classical philosophy and indicates how the political and educational theories of Plato and Aristotle were continued in different parts of ancient Christianity. Her feminist analysis suggests that the trend toward eliminating socially determined differences between women and men, based on reproductive function, which was initiated in the Jesus movement and in the early Paul, is reversed in later New Testament texts in order to conform to Greco-Roman patriarchal social structures.

Elisabeth Gössmann traces the construction of women's difference in the writings of the church fathers and mediaeval theologians who sought to integrate biblical thought with the philosophies of Platonism, Neoplatonism, Stoicism and Aristotelianism. From Augustine to the syntheses of scholasticism in the Middle Ages, the pattern is one of sharp dualism, in which the hope of Christian androcentric tradition is that in the eschaton women will become fully human, that is, men or at least 'like men'. To study the texts of this tradition of asymmetrical thought can help women and men today to think beyond the dualities and polarities of the past to a new and single principle of the human.

Sylvia Marcos uses a series of texts from ancient Mexico as a striking case-study of the feminist critiques of anthropology and ethnology. She concentrates on the intersection between gender and morality to provide insight into a pre-Christian society that did not affirm or legitimate rigid or mutually exclusive categories of distinction between the sexes. Genders fused in a dualism that was dynamic and ordered to balance and equilibrium. A positive attitude towards pleasure and sexuality was manifest in religion and everyday life. There is no implication in Aztec society that either sex is superior, but rather there is an awareness that each sex is different, difference being necessary for balance and equilibrium. The texts that Marcos examines reflect a society where the construction of gender is based on similarity rather than hierarchy.

In an illuminating account of Enlightenment and Romantic philosophies and related imaginative literature, Sarah Coakley undertakes a study of the idea of the 'man of reason' and eighteenth- and nineteenth-century appraisals of the distinctions between the sexes. She argues that the question that this complex legacy raises for Christian feminism is the integration, out of the resources of Christian history and spirituality, of sexual desire and desire for God. She shows the dependence of feminist thought on the Enlightenment heritage and questions whether its demands for global principles in ethics can be easily discarded today.

An article on the status of essentialism in feminist theory that we had hoped to include in this section failed to materialize. But readers will recognize that the postmodernist critique of essentialist thought and its concomitant celebration of women's difference would need to be taken into account. The theories of some of the French feminists, based on psychoanalysis and its 'linguistic turn', have been used to good advantage in some recent theological work and hold promise for future developments which attend to 'difference' in all its class, race, and ethnic aspects.

In our final section, there are three articles relating to specifically theological issues. Katherine Zappone reviews the question of theological anthropology from the perspective of the affirmation that women's difference from one another is as important as their difference from men. Her point is that women's (and men's) biology does affect their lives and destinies insofar as biology interacts with other elements: culture, race, geographical and historical situation. And Zappone argues that feminist thought must move beyond its fear of 'difference' as an analytic category that necessarily carries the implication of inferiority and inequality. The praxis of 'living with difference' in stepping outside the racial, sexual, cultural and class distinctions that one has inherited will emerge in a new solidarity that has significance for genuine and continued political change for the better for all women.

In a similar vein, Maria Clara Lucchetti Bingemer argues for a retrieval of the 'eternal feminine' in a constantly changing and liberative temporality or historicality. She shows both past and present appropriations of Mary of Nazareth in the church, pointing out distortions and possibilities in the symbol of Mary as it has functioned and can function for women. Arguing from a Latin American liberationist perspective, Luchetti Bingemer urges that while an 'eternal feminine' in the simple sense does not exist, there is new room for a provisional, diverse, multiple and contingent set of expressions of its meaning in different cultural contexts and historical periods as the access of the human to the eternal, transcendent and immanent God. She offers a feminist revisioning of God as loving and compassionate father and mother, as son and word incarnate in men and women, and as the productive and always surprising spirit of life in the lives of the poor.

In the final article, Elizabeth Johnson discusses the maleness of Christ and the historical misuse of this fact in Christian theology and practice. At the same time she shows that this maleness is open to liberating, feminist interpretation. She argues that the principle of one human nature in an interdependence of multiple differences moves beyond the models of sexual dualism or sameness of abstract individuals to the celebration of diversity as entirely normal. This is a multiple-term sequence in which connection in difference is central rather than identity through opposition or uniformity. Such an anthropology would allow christology to integrate the maleness of Christ in an undistorted way. Johnson offers interpretations of the mystery of the resurrection, wisdom christology and the biblical symbol of the body of Christ to expand the reality of Christ to include all of the redeemed and shows the significance of the baptism and martyrdom traditions for an inclusive christology.

It has been noted recently that the question of the 'nature of women' has become an international issue in the Roman Catholic Church. We believe that the articles in this number of *Concilium* demonstrate the diversity of new feminist theory and theology about the question of women's difference today and hope that this collection will elicit further thought and action in the international and interdependent community of women and men.

Anne Carr
Elisabeth Schüssler Fiorenza

Psychology instead of Theology?

A *dispute new and old*

'The issue in the case of Dr Drewermann is that of basic structures which have the utmost significance for the construction of theology but which cannot be demonstrated easily in a tangible way.' And elsewhere: 'What is at issue here is the foundation of biblical Christian belief.' With these remarks, on 7 October 1991, the President of the German Episcopal Conference, Bishop Dr K. Lehmann, seconded the Archbishop of Paderborn, Dr J.-J. Degenhardt, in his decision, published the same day, to withdraw from Dr Eugen Drewermann until further notice his authorization as a church teacher. Among the reasons given by Lehmann for this reprimand was that in the work of the theologian being disciplined, the radical new element of the Christian faith was no longer given its due because of his recourse to interpretations in terms of comparative religion. Rather, this radical new element was being put on the same level as the imagery of human and religious history, interpreted as archetypes. It was alleged that the concentration on the human subject and its inner experience neglected the fact that the Christian faith is indebted primarily to an event of revelation which takes place outside us. Bishop Lehmann stated: 'Drewermann, however, is largely interested only in the dimension of "inner truth". Thus he often arrives at misleading contrasts, as for example between "biological" and "symbolic". Drewermann often distorts and caricatures the reality of revelation – that God has entered bodily into our history.'

There should not and cannot be any question here of defending and evaluating Drewermann's extensive work, which at least in the German-speaking world has achieved best-seller status. Nor is it right and proper to relate yet again the long-drawn-out history of conflict between the Archbishop of Paderborn and the theologian whom he has now dismissed. Over and above all the complications which are closely connected with the persons concerned, this 'affair' has a more general significance. What is under discussion once again is the question of the relationship between theology and the modern human sciences, in this case psychology (depth psychology).

If the issue at stake is that psychological insights should not just be received superficially, say as 'techniques' for extending and improving the arsenal of pastoral methods, but really be integrated into theology in such a way as not to avoid the challenge which they present to traditional patterns of theological thought and conceptuality, then this inter-disciplinary discussion now seems to be fraught with a very high degree of conflict – especially in the sphere of the Catholic church. Indeed, anyone who sets out to establish links between the statements and symbols of the Christian tradition and the substance of the critical content of psychoanalytic experience, and thus really to understand the inner dimension of these statements and symbols, will have considerable difficulties with the technical theological language which has so far been customary and the categories that it tends to use.

However, it is short-sighted to regard such a concern to open up the Christian faith in a new way as a questioning or even a denial of the fundamentals of this faith and to reject the approach. Rather, here we have a contrast between fundamentally different ways of approaching the reality of faith which at first sight seem difficult to reconcile. However, they cannot be grasped adequately by the use of sweeping classifications like 'subjective versus objective' or 'symbolic versus historical'. Moreover it is even more fatal to suppose that one can use decisions of the *magisterium* to do away with such different approaches and the misconceptions that result from them.

It can be inferred from Drewermann's work to what degree and in what areas the critical discussion with psychology is a challenge to theology and calls for revisions to theology (though of course it must be noted that there is no such thing as 'psychology' by itself, any more than there is such a thing as 'theology' by itself). That is true, even if there are many questions that one might want to put to him on particular points. Nowhere else has this issue so far been worked out in such detail. Here is an attempt to use depth psychology to assess the whole territory of theology in respect of method and content. It is an impressive enterprise, even if in some respects it proves to be unmistakably one-sided. So it provides a basis for outlining at least the headings for some possible starting points for a fertile encounter between psychology (depth psychology) and particular theological issues. At the same time one can also note the problems which arise in this connection.

A first insight is the extent to which human consciousness and action are shaped and influenced by unconscious structures which are usually already formed and developed in early childhood; this development leads to obsessions and repressions, anxieties and guilt feelings. This raises a question for the moral preaching of the church. How helpful is it to appeal abstractly to human freedom and the capacity for insight – and thus also the capacity for guilt – on the assumption that human conduct can be orientated on commandments and norms which are supposed to be objectively valid? Not least, biblical examples can demonstrate that condemnations reinforce a tendency to externalization and inner alienation, while an approach concerned with understanding enables individuals gradually to free themselves from internalized forces and to develop a self strong enough to achieve self-determination. Whether that means that grace and law are mutually exclusive is a question which ethics must refer back to depth psychology.

A second insight is that symbols and mythical images have an indispensable power of their own. In enabling people to recall significant experiences, unfulfilled wishes and hopes, depth psychology can help us to understand and interpret the texts of the Bible in such a way that they are not just read as evidence of the faith-experiences of former generations, but provide illumination and healing for people today. Historical-critical exegesis yields important results in enabling the texts being investigated to be understood better as products of their time. But it remains inadequate when the concern is to bring their redemptive content to bear on the experiences of modern men and women. Precisely here, the depth-psychological interpretation can help by illuminating both the form and content of the texts as a concentrated expression of basic experiences (whether individual and biographical or universally human and collective) which affect people in the innermost depths of their existence. In this way it opens up access to the real truths of religious life. However, it would be dangerous for concentration on pastoral need to lessen the perception of structurally based human oppression and suffering in specific human histories.

A third insight is that while language is a necessary means of expression for self-understanding and communication between one self and another, it is not an adequate one. Depth psychology enlightens theology, especially dogmatics, about the possibilities and limitations of conceptual and didactic attempts to formulate and communicate the truths of revelation. This comes close to Augustine's view that the redemptive power of the Christian message can really be brought home and felt only where it succeeds in relating to the deepest levels of the human soul. The concern must then be for the traditional doctrinal content of the Christian faith constantly to be fused with an experiential content which people can understand. It cannot just be presented as 'external' doctrine. Against this background, we must again take up and discuss problems which have remained unresolved in Catholic theology since 'Modernism', like the definition of the relationship between experience and revelation – and do so without the threat of a verdict from the *magisterium*.

However, the lack of freedom accorded to the interdisciplinary discussion between theology and psychology (depth psychology) does not seem so much to be connected with the explosive nature of the fundamental themes and problems which are being addressed. The catalyst for the most recent conflict mentioned here may rather have been something else, namely the radical explanation given by depth psychology of the origin and function of domination and power as they appear in any social context, and its concern to overcome them by giving awareness and strength to the self in the face of any attempt to take charge of it or to direct it. From such a perspective this psychology undeniably provides stimuli which must seem dangerous, if not threatening, to a church which so far has found it difficult to acknowledge the freedom of Christians. So what is at issue in this new, old dispute about the relationship between psychology and theology is less the foundations of faith than apparently the question of power in the church. So far every effort has been made to prevent it from being raised and discussed openly.

Norbert Mette

I · 'Women's Difference' in Political, Social and Ecclesial Struggles

In Search of the Feminine Condition

A plea for a women's ecumene[1]

Ina Praetorius

1. Androcentric logic

'My' language is only mine with qualifications, because I am a woman. It embraces reality dualistically, in a specific way. Asymmetrical and opposed pairs structure perception. Rationality and emotion, public and private, knowledge and faith, intellectual work and manual work, Logos and myth, spirit and matter, God and man, master and slave, outside and inside, are related like husband and wife in patriarchal marriage. In each instance one of the two sides is defined as being of higher value than the other. So these essential structural polarities, which this language has moulded for centuries, are related like 'male' and 'female' in a patriarchal order.

Women must necessarily make use of this language which divides the world into an interesting male half and a trivial female half, at least if they want to be heard in public. If they want to be successful in specific political controversies, for example in the struggle over fair access to the necessities of life, they are asked to give answers to the question whether and to what extent they are 'the same as' men or 'different' from them. For the question of fair access to the necessities of life is at present usually articulated as the question of 'equal pay for equal work'. Women who can prove that they are 'the same' get their share, and the others stay inside: as dependents in the home, where work does not count as work and where as a result there is no possibility of earning anything worth mentioning. In the prevailing order, the question of equality or difference can initially amount only to whether women submit to the 'superior' which offers itself as a criterion for equality, or whether they accept the place among the others, the 'inferiors', which has long been assigned to them. For example, if a woman says that she regards women as being more sensitive or having more empathy than men because of their socialization or their 'nature', she is not making a neutral statement about women. Rather, she is assigning them irrefutably and perhaps against their will to an inferior realm.

2. Coping with patriarchal logic: spaces for women

It is humiliating if access to an existence which is fair to women – for example, to an existence without poverty – is regulated by such a primitive mechanism. But this is the patriarchal *status quo*, at least in the part of the world in which I live. Women are forced to go through the logic of 'the same as' or 'different from' (men) if they want to gain access to the spheres in which decisions are made about the distribution of the necessities of life like space, money and education. So they have to make use of a language within which an authentic expression of women's nature is impossible. For example, a woman who wants to stand for a seat in Parliament has to prove publicly that she can speak and argue 'as well as' men, though it may have long been clear to her that masculine rhetoric with its alleged objectivity and lack of emotion is a fraud. The way to most of the influential positions leads through 'equality' and thus in fact through adaptation to masculine standards.

Once women become aware that they are caught up in an alien logic, then the question of 'equality or difference' changes. We no longer look for statements about the *nature* of women in the prevailing terminology, since this quest cannot lead anywhere as long as androcentric presuppositions are not challenged. Rather, we look for a method by which we can escape the logic of equality without giving up our claims to liberation. We look for places in which and from which the prevalent logic – or the identification of women with it – can be neutralized. If there is to be any possibility of women using the logic of 'as good as/different from' (men) where necessary as an instrument for their liberation, instead of being subjected to it, they must have a home in places outside this logic. How can such places be rediscovered or created?

3. The roots of a policy of equal rights in the European Enlightenment

First of all it seems to me necessary to be convinced that there can be places outside the patriarchal order; that the predominant language is not the only proper one and that the prevailing situation is not the only possible one. In order to arrive at this conviction, I can ask some historical questions. Was it always like this? How did women get in the situation of being able to express themselves only as 'the same as' or 'different from' men, as the accepted criterion, i.e. inauthentically? My sketch of an answer to this question is limited to the cultural context to which I myself belong, since I think that it is probable that women in other contexts, for example in the East, would describe their history in relation to the dilemma of androcentric logic in a different way.

In Europe, at the latest since the Enlightenment, women have used the concept of equal rights to advance their liberation from unjust circumstances. This concept follows the programme of the Enlightenment. Faced with a feudal order, the Enlightenment proclaimed the equality of all human beings and derived far-reaching social programmes of reform from it. Initially many Enlightenment figures wanted these programmes also to include women. But because in fact to give women equal rights involved more far-reaching changes than any other reform in the name of equality, and because, as we now know, the basically androcentric concept of equality came up against logical barriers in the case of women, programmes for giving women equal rights were soon relegated to what was acceptable to patriarchy. Marriage law remained hierarchical, women were not given the vote, and universities were not open to those of the female sex.[2] Women who had hoped for more real progress from the Enlightenment joined the programme for equal rights. Only a few of them saw through the basically patriarchal structure of this concept, with its uninterrupted basic assumption of the masculine as the higher principle of equality and thus of the feminine.

The politics of equal rights achieved some of its goals: access to active and passive electoral rights, access to formal education, reforms in marriage law, and so on. But nowadays the real quality of life for women in the Western world is quite disproportionate to the immense efforts made and still being made by women in their programme to achieve equal rights: bruising battles for what should be a matter of course; the many burdens associated with the traditional work of women added on to the demand for adaptation to male standards of achievement. In the 'Christian West', patriarchy has not been made aware of its limitations, but has incorporated the potential of these women who are 'on equal terms' into its aims, which seem all the more globally destructive, the more they go on. Women who have fought for equal status – usually women from the middle and upper classes – play a part in the patriarchal praxis of exploitation of the 'Third World', of nature and of marginalized groups within their own society. Women who cannot, or do not want to, achieve this status, are still numbered among the poor.[3]

As a result of this, feminists today are asking whether the Enlightenment concept of equality for women was really progress, or whether the slogan of equality was not rather a lamentable substitute for the women's culture which was systematically destroyed in Europe in the course of the persecution of witches. Might it not be a consequence of what was perhaps a unique campaign of the annihilation of women and their culture that above all European and North American women, in a situation of isolation, have dissociated themselves from the deceptive ideal of equality and thus from an alien ideal of freedom? And if that is the case, how, in modern conditions, can women clear the rubble away from spaces in which they can *mutually* safeguard their dignity and their strength?

4. Elements of a theory of women's relationships

Nowadays, women theorists from various backgrounds[4] are working on the question how an independent women's culture can be established outside the patriarchal order or how the existing women's culture which is either not valued or devalued can be brought to light and given value. Their work is based on the insight that an effective subversion of patriarchal culture can come into being more readily from independent feminine complexes of culture and tradition than from a 'policy of demands' based on a principle of equality.[5] If I see things rightly, all these theoretical approaches, which are at present being vigorously discussed in Europe and North America, have a number of structural elements in common.

1. They begin from an analysis of the prevailing order, in which women are fixated on male relationships – on heterosexuality in a comprehensive sense. When Janice Raymond talks of 'hetero-reality', Adrienne Rich of 'compulsory heterosexuality', Sarah Lucia Hoagland of 'heterosexualism' and the women involved in the Milan 'Women's Library' talk of 'male genealogy', by and large they mean the same thing. Women are imprisoned in a social and symbolic order which fixates women on the male as their real and symbolic counterpart, and so isolates them from one another. Consequently, 'equality' can only mean equality with the male. In their analyses all female theorists conclude that this order not only damages women but also bears some responsibility for the catastrophic state of the world: for ecological catastrophe, for armaments and war. By making themselves the criterion of all things and all people, men (some men?) subject *other* forms of life to the possibility of global destruction.

2. Starting from this analysis, these theorists postulate a move by women towards women: not as a random preference, but as a revolutionary action. If women turn their attention away from males and begin to perceive, name and evaluate one another, then the patriarchal order will collapse. For males are dependent on the confirmation and admiration of 'their' women and on the male-centred work of women in the background.

3. The starting point of all female theorists is that there have long been strong relationships between women. Adrienne Rich talks of a 'lesbian continuum' in which all women are in fact involved, in that they are daughters of mothers and often mothers of daughters; in so far as they are looked after by women as long as they are children and as soon as they are sick or old; in so far as they have relationships with women as friends. So it is less a matter of creating relationships between women out of nothing than above all of naming them and thus giving them value, writing their history and discovering their potentially revolutionary function. What is unspokenly already there is to be recognized and consciously conceived of as a valuable form of life.

4. In almost all sketches, the explicitly lesbian form of life plays an essential role as a model and a point of orientation. It as it were takes the place which is occupied by monogamous marriage in the patriarchal order. Without elevating the lesbian pattern of life to be the only one worth striving for, by this reorientation of values women make their central concern clear: the fixation on the male, which finds classical expression in the order of monogamous marriage, is done away with in favour of orientation on a binding relationship between women.

5. All female authors associate the personal dimension of relationships between women with the political dimension, and the intellectual dimension with the physical everyday dimension. Relationships between women cannot only be personal, if the disruptive potential inherent in them is taken seriously. On the other hand, the ideal towards which these women are moving is not that of purely pragmatic alliances between women, without an emotional quality. The political and the personal spheres overlap.

In these five common structural elements I see a kind of guideline for future feminist reflection and action which can lead out of the barren alternative of 'the same as/different from'. I think that a feminist theory and praxis with this aim must in fact go through the five stages outlined above: the recognition of the closed androcentrism of 'our' culture and its catastrophic consequences; the recognition that an authentic self-expression on the part of women is possible only if we escape this logic by relating to one another; the insight that if we want to attach value to women and their relationships with one another, we must not stand in a void, but see this as a history which has been covered over, and recognize the need to give expression to an 'unreflected-on presence';[6] the radical questioning of an image of human beings which rests on the 'natural complementing of each other' by the sexes, and consequently the breaking down of anxieties about lesbian forms of life and reservations about them; and finally, deliberate action in overcoming the asymmetrical dualisms which seek to divide our life into a private half and a public half.

5. A field of work for the future: definitions of the feminine condition which transcend frontiers

What still does not seem to me to be being discussed with sufficient intensity in European and probably also North American feminism is how the women's culture which is postulated can come to transcend frontiers, or, to be more precise, how we can work on forms of discrimination existing between women which are rooted in structures. Racism, class rule, antisemitism, Eurocentrism and other forms of discrimination stand in the way of a women's culture of dialogue which transcends frontiers. If women want to discover who they are as women and what ideas they have – possibly in common – about a life which is fair to women, and if they want to detach their definition of themselves and the world from the male criterion which is supposedly universal, it is important to extend the discussion beyond their own group. For women, too, run the risk of stylizing their own limited experiences as the feminine condition.

It is clear that white women from the middle classes in highly industrialized countries have already succumbed to this danger, and that as a result barren misunderstandings and divisions have come into being in the women's movement. But if the concept of equality which has so far been dominant in Western women's movements has now proved questionable, that alone is reason enough to stop maintaining, as many Western feminists do – often tacitly – that Western feminism is the most 'progressive'. Perhaps women from cultures in which (relatively) autonomous women's cultures have remained more intact than in Europe and North America – and these are cultures which Western feminists often describe as 'backward' – may take on a pioneering role. For perhaps they may make more important contributions to the question of a non-androcentric feminine self-understanding from women's traditions that really exist than those which are more markedly alienated from themselves as the result of a long struggle for 'equality'. But whether this is the case can only be decided by a real discussion, not by speculation at a European desk.

I think that it is important to pay more attention to feminist dialogue which transcends frontiers, not only because the global expansion of Western patriarchy compels us to engage in global collaboration but also because it is interesting and enjoyable to investigate the feminine conditions with other women from other contexts. As it does not function automatically – on the basis of the assumption of a universal sisterhood – it too should be the object of careful theoretical study in the same way as relationships between women within a single cultural group have come to be of interest to the women theorists I have mentioned. If women want to devote themselves to this very comprehensive and labour-intensive task, however, they must take the decisive step that those who have produced theories on relationships between women postulate and have perhaps already taken: they must have decided to give discourse among women priority over dialogue with males. For me, as a Western Christian woman theologian, that means, for example, looking at my own use of time. How much of my limited time do I devote to critical discussion with my own androcentric tradition – and thus to a male-dominated discourse – and how much to discussion with women from other contexts? If I have discovered the priority of the other woman for my and our self-assurance, then any discussion with androcentric traditions which does not have as its criterion understandings with other women will become superfluous.

6. A vision

I can imagine women from the different world religions, from different political systems and cultural traditions, coming together in women's ecumenical networks. They do not necessarily need a patriarchal supra-structure to do that. Conference centres and world assemblies are unnecessary, since our societies are already multi-cultural. I can travel to distant lands, but I do not need to do so in order to enter into a conversation with other women about what distinguishes us from one another and what binds us together. The decisive thing is my wish and that of the other woman to find each other in a shared conversation.

I can imagine women who have found themselves in such networks spending a good deal of time discussing carefully, in critical solidarity, suggestions which have already been made, or which will be made in the future, about a definition of their being in this world. The discussion might include a statement like this: 'Women must recognize what they have in common, even if they make very different decisions. However they may estimate their capacity for bearing children, at all events it is the case that freedom in their lives has no concrete significance as long as they do not live

in conditions which make it possible to shape this freedom themselves.'[7]
Or this: 'We are really all similar by virtue of the fact that we carry around
with us a difference in sex which we have not reflected on, and which is the
foundation of our being like one another.'[8]

I can imagine women enjoying such an encounter. They are increasingly
attracting others. One day they will agree on guidelines and key terms by
which all will be able to express themselves while nevertheless remaining
different from others who are also expressing themselves in these words.
They will be supported by these words and statements if – as for the
moment seems unavoidable – they continue their policy of demanding an
existence which is fair to women. They will have found a place from which
it is possible to *play* equality when that is necessary, a place where liberated
(instead of spiteful) laughter is possible about what males once dared to
offer us as the supreme goal: equality.

Translated by John Bowden

Notes

1. This article arises out of critical discussions in solidarity with women from the
'Ethics in Feminism' project: † Marianne Briner, Ruth Egloff, Andrea Günter,
Sigrun Holz, Rose Killinger, Beatrix Schiele, Jacqueline Sonego-Moser and Heidrun
Suter-Richter.
2. For this see Ursula Pia Jauch, *Immanuel Kant zur Geschlechterdifferenz.
Aufklärerische Vorurteilskritik und bürgerliche Geschlechtsvormundschaft*, Vienna
1988.
3. For the concept of poverty presupposed here see Enrique Dussel, *Ethik der
Gemeinschaft*, Düsseldorf 1988, 31f.
4. E.g. Libreria delle donne di Milano, *Wie weibliche Freiheit entsteht. Eine neue
politische Praxis*. Berlin ²1988; Diotima, *Philosophinnengruppe aus Verona. Der
Mensch ist zwei. Das Denken der Geschlechterdifferenz*, Vienna 1989; Sarah Lucia
Hoagland, *Lesbian Ethics. Toward New Value*, Palo Alto 1988; Janice G. Raymond,
Frauenfreundschaft. Philosophie der Zuneigung, Munich 1986; Adrienne Rich,
'Zwangsheterosexualität und lesbische Existenz', in Elisabeth List and Herlinde Studer
(eds.), *Denkverhältnisse. Feminismus und Kritik*, Frankfurt am Main 1989, 244–78.
Section 4 relates to these texts.
5. Libreria delle donne (n.4), 26.
6. Cf. Adriana Cavarero, 'Ansätze zu einer Theorie der Geschlechterdifferenz', in
Diotima (n.4), 65–102.
7. Beverly Wildung Harrison, *Our Right to Choose. Toward a New Ethic of Abortion*,
Boston 1983, 36.
8. Cavarero, 'Ansätze' (n.6), 96.

Women's Difference and Equal Rights in the Church

Rosemary Radford Ruether

The full incorporation of women into the ministry of the Christian churches has become the critical issue for Christianity today. How churches handle this issue may well determine whether they survive as viable religious options for humanity in the future. Christianity inherits from its historical past a fundamental contradiction in its views and treatment of one half of humanity, women. On the one hand, Christianity, from its beginnings, has committed itself to a universalist soteriological egalitarianism. All human beings, regardless of gender, class or ethnicity, are created by God and saved by Christ. Salvation knows no distinction between human beings.

On the other hand, Christian understanding of the nature of being, both of God and Christ and of normative humanity, has been cast in male generic terms. This male generic understanding of being has been used to subordinate women, both as members of humanity and as persons capable of exercising authority and representing God and Christ. The exclusion of women from ordained ministry, and indeed from all public leadership in past Christian societies, has been rooted in this male generic understanding of human and divine being.

Only in the present century have women gained access to political rights in society and to higher education and so have been, for the first time, in a position to challenge these exclusions from Christian leadership in the churches. By and large, liberal societies have been ahead of the churches in recognizing women's rights as full human persons, although there are still many issues that remain unresolved in the social arena. This fact has been used by some conservatives to claim that the whole issue of women's rights in the church is inappropriate. They claim that feminism is the importation into the churches of a purely 'secular' issue.[1]

However, this separation of religion and secular society in regard to sexism is misleading. The male dominant patterns in Christianity originate from a time when the church and patriarchal society were integrally related, when the church borrowed patterns of organization from patriarchal society and buttressed those patterns with theological symbolism and argumentation. The issue of women's subordination is both social and religious. It is a part of the heritage of secular and theological ideologies. The churches must deal with this issue both in terms of ecclesiastical organization and in terms of theology.

Liberal Protestant churches, over the last 130 years and particularly the last 30 years, have changed their practices and begun to ordain women. But most of them were not prepared to recognize that this change demanded a rethinking of theological symbolism and ecclesiastical organization. Consequently, women have been integrated into ministry in token numbers and in low-paid, marginal positions in a system that still symbolizes human and especially divine being as male. This, of course, is not unlike the treatment of women in secular culture and society.[2]

In Catholicism the celibate clerical system of ministry is in crisis. Laywomen, especially nuns, are doing an increasing proportion of the actual ministry of the church, but without official recognition as ordained ministers. The Vatican has mobilized itself against any liberalization in the areas of reproductive rights and the ordination of women.

The American Catholic bishops are caught in the middle between rising women's consciousness in the church and this Vatican intransigence. This is true of many other national episcopacies as well. On the one hand, the bishops recognize that they cannot do without women. Women are both the majority of the active churchgoers and the majority of the volunteer workers in the church. An increasing share of the professional, that is, paid, ministry is done by women.

The bishops are tied to the Vatican by a system of universal jurisdiction and appointment of bishops that was created by nineteenth-century ultramontanism. This means that bishops lack the independence to challenge the Vatican on any critical matters of doctrinal or moral teaching in such areas as reproductive rights and ordination. Even the question of artificial birth control, which was actually settled, as far as the consensus of moral theologians and of laity goes, twenty years ago, remains unchanged in official teaching.[3]

The drafts of the American bishops' pastoral letter on women reveal these contradictions all too painfully.[4] On the one hand, the episcopal authors of the letter attempted to give full rhetorical affirmation to the legitimacy of women's concerns for full equality in society and in the church. They condemned in no uncertain terms the 'sins of sexism that violate the basic tenets of our faith'. But their ability to follow up these words with practical changes in areas such as reproductive rights, support for the Equal Rights Amendment, or ordination of women, is totally lacking. The structures that tie women to subordinate positions in society and in the church remain largely in place.

The bishops took as their theological starting-point the scriptural text, Genesis 1.27, which says that 'man' is created in the image of God, male and female. They take for granted that this text means, and has always meant, the equality of men and women. This ignores the fact that for most of the history of Christian tradition this text was interpreted asymmetrically. That is, it was understood to mean that the male possesses the image of God normatively, and women are included in the image of God only under the male as their head.[5]

More recent Catholic anthropology moved from arguments about women's natural inferiority to arguments for women's difference and complementary relations to males. In the first draft the bishops disregarded the anthropologies of subordination and of complementarity. They adopted an anthropology of equivalence and partnership of equals between men and women in the family, in society, and in the church. However, they seem to have been caught up short by the Vatican and more conservative American Catholic bishops. As was evident from the Pope's statement on the 'Dignity and Vocation of Women' (August 1988), he favours an anthropology of complementarity that divides males and females into two opposite psycho-symbolic ontologies.[6]

The inability of the American bishops to affirm any real peer relations of men and women becomes explicit when we turn to the question of the participation of men and women in the ministry of the church. In their pastoral letter, all the bishops were able to offer was an increased participation of women in the ministry of the laity. The ordained clergy remains an all-male preserve. They endorse the position of the 1976 Vatican Declaration (reaffirmed by John Paul II in his letter) against the ordination of women which declared that women are ontologically incapable of being ordained because they cannot image Christ.[7] Both the Pope and the bishops seem oblivious to the contradiction between this statement and their own theological starting point of equality of men and women in the image of God.

The inability of the American Catholic bishops to carry through their theological starting-point of women's equality in creation ends in a contradiction of this theological starting-point. Women are said to be fully equal to men in the image of God and yet incapable of imaging Christ.

What is the root of this contradiction? How can it be that bishops, who presume to be the primary theological teachers of the church, do not recognize such blatant contradiction between their theological anthropology and their christology?

The roots of this contradiction lie in the 1976 Vatican Declaration itself which attempted to create just such a schism between anthropology and christology. This Declaration attempted to separate the issue of women's civil equality in society from ordination. It asserted that the Catholic Church (the *magisterium*) had always supported women's civil equality, but that the question of women's ordination is not a question of civil rights or equality in the natural order, but belongs to a separate and higher plane of sacramental relations between the church and God. In effect, what this does is to separate the created or natural order and the sacramental order or order of grace into two different spheres unrelated to each other. Women are said to be equal in the natural order of creation, but this has no implications for the ecclesial or sacramental order of salvation.

Interestingly, this dualism partly reverses the classical view taken by the church fathers, in which women were presumed to be unequal and fundamentally inferior in nature, but equal in the order of grace. The church fathers thought of women as lacking equality in the image of God and as being under the headship of the male in the created order. But in Christ this inequality had been annulled. In the language of Galatians 3.28, in Christ there is neither male nor female.

Classical Christianity suffered from a contradiction between its creational anthropology and its christology, but in the opposite direction. Women were presumed to be unequal in nature. This inequality dictated the temporal structure of the church as patriarchal. But on the plane of salvation, which anticipated heaven, this patriarchal hierarchy of man over women had been annulled. How do we seem to have developed to a reversed view in modern Catholic teaching, in which women become equal in nature or creation (secular society), but unequal in grace (in Christ and in the Church)?

Basically, this has come about because civil societies in the West have moved to grant women civil equality. Contrary to the Vatican Declaration, this reform was not supported by the Pope or the bishops when it was happening. In fact, both opposed women's suffrage when this struggle was going on in the first part of the twentieth century.[8] But this history is conveniently forgotten. The Catholic *magisterium* (more or less) concedes to women this new arena of civil equality. This means that it also changes its previous teaching that women are unequal in nature to men. It declares itself to have 'always taught' that women are equal to men in nature. This means that, in order to defend the tradition of excluding women from ordination, it must invent a new distinction between the natural and the sacramental planes.

This hierarchical ordering of nature and grace echoes the scholastic or Thomistic tradition, but it contradicts Thomas's own understanding. In the teaching of Thomas Aquinas, women were fundamentally unequal in nature. He borrowed the false biology of Aristotle to declare that women were defective or 'misbegotten' humans who lacked full normative human nature. For this reason they could not represent human nature in any leadership position in society. Only the male could represent full or normative human nature.[9]

Thomas's christology and theology of priesthood followed this patriarchal anthropology. Since only men possessed full, normative human nature, it followed that Christ had to be male to possess the fullness of humanness. Only men in turn could represent Christ in the priesthood. Thomas's patriarchal construction of anthropology, christology and priesthood were coherent. Only on the soteriological level did Thomas diverge from this patriarchal construction. In keeping with ancient Christian tradition he assumes that this inequality of women is overcome by the grace of salvation won by Christ. Thus women are included in salvation, despite their incapacity for full humanness.

This Thomistic tradition is the root of the startling statement in the 1976 Vatican Declaration which claimed that women cannot be ordained because they do not image Christ. But the Vatican Declaration attempts to eliminate the anthropological roots of this theological viewpoint. Women's inability to image Christ now hangs in the air as a matter of sacramental symbolism alone, no longer based on natural inferiority.

One can only wonder, then, whether the other pole of the relationship is now in jeopardy. If the maleness of Christ now becomes a limitation of grace rather than nature, does this mean that women, in fact, are not equally included in grace? If women's inability to image Christ lies in the realm of grace, rather than nature, does this mean that the grace won by Christ no longer equally includes women? If women cannot represent Christ, how does Christ represent women? Or, to put it another way, if women cannot be ordained, then they cannot be baptized either.

What all this means is that the church is challenged in a new way today to make coherent sense out of its theology, to bring together its anthropology, its christology and its soteriology. If women are understood to be equal both in nature and in grace, there is no longer any basis for declaring that they cannot represent Christ sacramentally. The flight back to an anthropology of complementarity, and the abandonment of the anthropology of equivalence in the second draft of the American bishops' pastoral, seeks to evade this issue. The result is a reactionary document that makes no positive contributions to the issues and should be rejected altogether.[10]

As Roman Catholic patriarchalism loses its social basis in patriarchal feudal society, and faces instead societies which are, in theory if not in practice, democratic and egalitarian, there has been an increasing temptation to support its traditional social patterns inherited from the past by self-enclosed dogmatism. The church's social pattern no longer has the larger society as its reference and so can no longer argue that these patterns derive from the 'natural order', as Thomas Aquinas might have in the thirteenth century. In order to maintain these patterns, the church now sacramentalizes an archaic patriarchal and monarchical social system, making it appear to be a special expression of divine ordering of the church, apart from and unconnected with society. This self-enclosed authoritarianism was expressed in the dogma of infallibility, which was promulgated in 1870 at precisely the moment when the Catholic Church was losing its relation to feudal Catholic society and facing new democratic societies.

The Second Vatican Council appeared to promise a change in this self-enclosed dogmatism. But the present papacy is making a major and total assault on these developments and attempting to reassert a system of power rooted in self-enclosed monarchical infallibilism. This system of power no longer acknowledges any need to base itself on consultation with the rest of the church at any level, from bishops to priests to lay people. If there is to be any future for the Catholic church or ecumenical relations between Catholics and Protestants, this retrenchment of papal absolutism must be resisted. No church teaching can stand which does not possess an authentic consensus of the people.

Thus, the question of women's ordination, or indeed the discussion of any development in church teaching, opens up the deeper question of authority in the church. Catholicism stands today at the crossroads between two directions. It can either take the direction of Vatican II and progress toward a more authentic participatory community, in which all members are given a voice, or it can retreat in the direction of Vatican I and seek to restore papal absolute monarchy. This latter direction can only create a dwindling Roman sect, not a Catholic church. Women and men who are self-respecting of their own humanity will increasingly desert such a church.

The question of how Catholic feminists seek to find ways of participating in local churches, parishes and religious congregations is of critical importance. What sort of things can we and should we try to do in the light of the ambiguous and increasingly limited efforts of the American Catholic bishops to widen the space for women's ministries?

Women should move in and occupy any space for ministry that is opened to them and seek to make it liveable space. This means insisting on decent working conditions, legally and humanly. That is to say, reasonable contracts and remuneration and shared decision-making. But we should do this with our eyes wide open to the spiritual dangers of patriarchal working conditions. These conditions are dangerous to our spiritual health. So one should not put one's whole life and soul into such communities, but also create alternative free communities of spiritual nurture and support.[11] Both of these options need to exist side by side, if we are to survive spiritually and help the institutional church to reform.

We need to find creative ways to bring institutional and free communities into interaction so that they can enliven each other, rather than assuming that they are mutually exclusive options. Institutional churches typically offer two alternatives, either to conform to their limits or to leave as isolated individuals. We need to refuse both options. Instead, we need to establish new ground on the outside edge of historical communities, while retaining a base on the inside edge of these communities. In this way one has the freedom for new creativity, while taking over and using institutional resources to develop and communicate these projects. Christian feminists need to find the creative ways to make use of this dialectical strategy of transformation of culture and social structures, refusing to be either isolated or co-opted.

Oppressive power relations will not disappear in any institution completely. Moreover, the capacity for such oppressive power relations is in ourselves, as much as in our opponents. We are all in the process of continual conversion. What we need to work for here and now is not perfection, but good working and living space for ourselves and for one another. Wherever we can do something concretely to extend such good living space for ourselves and for some others, that is worth doing. Whatever we can do to shape communities where love and prophetic witness are at least glimpsed, that is worth doing. That is fundamentally what ministry and what being the church of Christ is all about.

Notes

1. William Oddie, *What Will Happen to God: Feminism and the Reconstruction of Christian Belief*, London 1984.

2. Jackson W. Carroll, Barbara Hargrove, Adair T. Lummiss, *Women of the Cloth: A New Opportunity for the Churches*, San Francisco 1981.

3. Robert Blair Kaiser, *The Politics of Sex and Religion*, Kansas City 1985.

4. The first draft, released in March 1988, was titled 'Partners in the Mystery of

Redemption'. The second draft, released on 5 April 1990, was titled 'One in Christ Jesus: A Pastoral Response to the Concerns of Women for Church and Society'.

5. The ambiguities of the inclusion and exclusion of women from the image of God in traditional Christian theology is explored in *Image of God and Gender Models*, ed. Kari Borresen, Oslo 1991.

6. John Paul II, 'The Dignity and Vocation of Women', 15 August 1988.

7. Congregation for the Doctrine of the Faith, 'Declaration on the Question of the Admission of Women to the Ministerial Priesthood', 15 October 1976.

8. See Rosemary Radford Ruether, *Contemporary Roman Catholicism: Crises and Challenges*, Kansas City 1987, 36–7, 79 n.22.

9. Thomas Aquinas, *Summa Theologica*, I, 92.

10. There has been a general condemnation of the second draft of the pastoral by progressive American Catholic women's groups. Even Bishop Rembert Weakland of Milwaukee, Wisconsin, called for the pastoral to be dropped as counter-productive. See Rosemary Ruether, 'Dear Bishops, You Insult our Intelligence', *National Catholic Reporter*, 18 May 1990, 16.

11. Rosemary Radford Ruether, *Women-Church: Theology and Practice of Feminist Liturgical Communities*, San Francisco 1986.

The Image of the 'White Lady': Gender and Race in Christian Mission

Kwok Pui-lan

The nineteenth century has been called by church historians the 'great century of Christian mission'. Christianity was brought to many parts of the world simultaneously with the rapid expansion of the West and colonialization of Third World countries. The missionary movement has been interpreted in conflicting ways according to different perspectives. Some emphasize the benevolent role of missionaries in introducing the gospel, Christian reform, and Western civilization to non-Western societies. Others criticize the missionary enterprise as culturally imperialistic, supporting the political and economic interests of Western colonial powers.

In the past debate on Christian mission, the role played by women in the missionary movement has not been sufficiently explored. In fact, Christian mission expanded during the latter half of the nineteenth century with the proliferation of women's mission and reform societies on both sides of the Atlantic. A significant part of mission funding came from donations by women in the church. Through sending women missionaries to work among the 'heathen', Western women established important links with women in other parts of the world. In the mission field, the missionary ladies preached not only the gospel but also the Western ideals of womanhood. In their home base, they helped to shape Western women's ideas about Third World women through their letters, reports and the bulk of missionary literature.

This article examines the myth and reality behind the image of the 'white lady' in Christian mission and Western colonialism. Exploring the interaction of gender and race constructions in the encounter between the West and other cultures, it raises important questions of identity and difference among women in cross-cultural perspective.

Women missionaries and Christian mission

Before examining the image of the 'white lady' in detail, it is important to discuss the social and cultural reasons for sending women as missionaries. In the beginning, only men were sent as missionaries to foreign lands. If they were accompanied by their wives, the ladies were expected to take care of responsibilities at home and the children. Sometimes these missionary wives would also assist mission work by visiting women at their homes and running small mission schools. It was considered too dangerous to send women to travel and work alone in a strange and unfamiliar land.

The need to send women missionaries arose because in some countries, such as China and India, the two sexes were segregated in society. Social propriety made it improper for male missionaries to approach women. Anti-Christian propaganda often portrayed male missionaries as having a craving sexual appetite and using charms and medicine pills to gain access to women.[1] Therefore, women missionaries had to be sent to work among women, who were reported as much more receptive to mission work than men. It was hoped that these women, once converted to Christianity, would influence their families and bring up their children in the Christian way. In addition, white female missionaries were considered to be less threatening than the white men. In places where antipathy towards Christian mission was exceptionally strong, white women were sent as pioneers to open the mission field.

The demand for female missionaries received a favourable response from the women's mission boards, newly formed in Europe and America. The upsurge of interest in missionary activities was fuelled by religious fervour brought about by the evangelical revival movement. At the same time, white women also deemed it their duty to save their 'heathen' sisters from their degraded and lowly position. In 1869, when the Congregationalist women in the United States organized the women's board, an appeal was issued to Christian women which said: 'Can there be anything more appropriate than for woman, elevated by the gospel to the high position she holds in Christian lands, to extend the helping hand to woman "sitting in the region and shadow of death" – ignorant, degraded, and perishing for lack of vision?'[2] Similar rhetoric was frequently found in missionary literature to solicit support and funds for mission.

At first, there was some hesitation about sending single women to the mission field for fear that they could not take care of themselves in foreign lands without the protection of their families. But the single ladies showed that they could share living quarters and form a supportive network of their own. Without family burdens, they could devote more time and energy to mission work and travel around as itinerants. The female missionaries were chiefly responsible for 'woman's work' in Christian mission, consisting of evangelism, female education and medical service. Mission work was divided distinctly along the gender line because of the segregation of the sexes.

The number of single women sent as missionaries by the women's boards continued to increase in the latter half of the nineteenth century. Together with the missionary wives, the total number of women in a particular mission field might even outnumber that of men. The feminization of the mission force was clearly evident, for example, in China. Although sent and supported by the women's boards, the female missionaries were supervised by the male missionaries in charge of a particular mission. In some denominations, missionary women could not perform leadership roles similar to those of men. Tension existed in some missions, where missionary women were not content with their subordinate position and demanded more control of their work. They also criticized the male missionaries for overlooking the importance of the distinct component of 'woman's work' in Christian mission.

The 'white lady' in mission: myth and reality

The white missionary women who travelled long distances to save their 'heathen' sisters were portrayed almost as saints in missionary literature and their 'hagiographic' biographies. It was true that many of these women were prompted by a strong religious conviction to join the Christian mission, but the mission field also provided opportunities not readily available at home. A study of the social background of American women missionaries at the turn of the century indicates that a high percentage of them came from middle-class families in small towns in the Midwest.[3] The newly-opened female colleges in America also provided a growing number of graduates who might not find an appropriate job easily on the home front. A missionary career in a foreign land offered new challenges and freedom denied to them in their own societies.

Motivated by their religious zeal and enchanted by the possibilities abroad, young white women dedicated themselves to be missionaries in the name of self-denial and sacrifice. Yet, the mission field offered them unexpected authority and power, contrary to their own beliefs of feminine subordination. They could lead an independent life, pursuing a career as teacher, doctor, or missionary. In a colonial or semi-colonial situation they enjoyed privileges and commanded respect as members of the white race. The historian Jane Hunter, who has studied American women missionaries in China, describes how these white ladies adjusted themselves to this new environment:

> At first they were troubled by the discrepancy between their expected demeanour of modesty and self-effacement, and their experience of authority. Gradually, however, the experience of authority transformed self-expectations, and missionary women came to discover inner certainties to match their circumstances. Gradually, they developed colonial temperaments to accord with their colonial status.[4]

Living in a foreign place, some of these women missionaries learned the language and tried to adjust themselves to local customs. But a greater number would stick to the Western habit of life rather than living like the local people. Many continued to wear Western dresses, although they were not suitable for the hot climate and inconvenient for travel. They lived in the mission compounds and decorated their homes as they did their homes in the West, with pieces of furniture and sometimes even an organ shipped across the ocean. These women missionaries tried to maintain their identity not only because they were homesick and wished to live in the traditional way, but also because of the privileges associated with it. The fact that they lived differently from the common people increased their appeal. For example, many village women were curious to have a look at a foreign woman, and they would touch her clothes, or visit her to see how she lived.

The female missionaries often assumed a self-styled mothering role in their relationship with native Christians. In their letters and writings, they referred to those under their instruction and supervision as 'children', even though these people were adults. They often established close emotional bonding with women and girls under their tutelage and sought to influence them through personal ties. But just like any mother, missionary women sometimes found that their 'daughters' could act in ways beyond their expectation and control. When in 1872 Mary Porter, a missionary in China, demanded that girls in her school unbind their feet, she could not have expected what this would lead to: 'The best result of the unbinding of feet in the Peking school was not foreseen by the missionaries. The girls, by submitting to this break with established custom . . . learned to think and act for themselves.'[5] Later, other missionary women were also surprised to see their students participate in mass demonstrations and nationalistic activities against foreign domination and colonialism.

As white women enjoying power and privilege, they related to men of a different race in an ambiguous way. On the one hand, their independence and status allowed them to break from certain gender stereotypes prescribed in their home countries. On the other hand, they found Asian or African men smaller in size and less masculine than Western men. Although sensitivity, gentleness and moderation were virtues valued by the Christian tradition, white women considered men of colour who displayed such qualities as unmanly or timid according to their Western gender expectations. White women sometimes called their male students 'lads', and their servants 'boys', just like the blacks at home.[6] They harboured ambivalent feelings on seeing these young 'lads' being ordained one day, preaching from the pulpit, and exercising ecclesiastical duties which they, as women, were barred from performing.

The encounter with a different social and cultural ethos made missionaries more aware of how women were treated in various contexts. They emphasized that Christianity had contributed to the uplift of women in the West, whereas heathenism and superstition were causes of the degradation of women in other parts of the world. In a book called *Women in All Lands*, an American missionary Young J. Allen remarked that the best single test of the civilization of any people is the degree to which their women are free and educated.[7] The prevalence of footbinding, concubinage, seclusion of women and female illiteracy was taken as a sign and symptom of the inferiority of other cultures. Within an unshakeable belief in their own cultural superiority, Allen and other missionaries stressed that other countries should take heed of the benefits of Christian civilization to transform their culture and society.

Female missionaries believed that Christianity accorded them a higher status in society and that they had the responsibility for imparting the 'Christian ideal of womanhood' through Christian schools and the example of missionary households. As products of their own time, these women missionaries perceived the 'Christian ideal of womanhood' as being not much different from their own Victorian values of domesticity and subordination. For example, they prescribed that women should have 'refined and womanly qualities', keeping their homes comfortable and clean. Wives should win respect from their husbands through their intelligence and learning, and they should handle relations with in-laws to the satisfaction of all. As enlightened mothers, they should treat their children conscientiously, judiciously, and with self-control. Displaying less tolerance towards the indigenous ideals of womanhood, female missionaries wished to transmit their own life-style, social manners and cultural values to their 'heathen' sisters.

The original purpose of their missionary career was to save feminine souls. Judging from their own standards, however, missionary women found that their sisters could not possibly be 'saved' without adopting some of their customs and values, such as monogamy, the nuclear family and female education.[8] At the turn of the century, mission ideology shifted from converting individual souls to regenerating 'heathen' culture through the transmission of Western civilization and institutions. Female missionaries played their part by introducing female education, Christian reform, the temperance movement, the YWCA and Western medicine to other cultures.

Compared with other radical women who were fighting for women's rights back home, women missionaries were generally considered more conservative in their political outlook. It seems ironic that they should have taken upon themselves the responsibility of advocating women's emancipation in the mission field. The historian Alison R. Drucker has tried to provide a plausible explanation: 'It was less disturbing to criticize another culture for injustice to women than to castigate one's own; religious women frequently avowed that introducing Christianity to the heathen would raise the status of women abroad.'[9] In order to justify their work, missionary reports focussed invariably on the pitiful condition of women of other lands and their immense needs. This missionary literature, widely read by church women in the nineteenth century, tended to reinforce the belief of uncritical readers in their own cultural superiority.

Gender, race and Christian mission

The study of Christian mission reveals the complex juxtaposition of gender, cultural superiority and religious identity. Mission ideology emphasized the essential difference between the white women and women of colour: the former as liberated because of their Christian religion; the latter as ignorant and degraded in their heathenism. Other cultures were understood to be diametrically opposite and hierarchically inferior to Western culture, and the subordination of women was taken as one sign or manifestation of this inferiority. Such beliefs could be used to justify the ecclesial interest of Christian mission, and also the ethnocentrism of the West.

To maintain such a mission ideology, the 'white lady' had to be mystified, so that she could be put on top of a pedestal. The struggle of Western women against the male power structure of the church in the first wave of feminism in the nineteenth century could not be told. The limitation and oppression of the Victorian conception of true womanhood has not been examined in missionary literature. On the other hand, the life and reality of women of colour was misrepresented in this social construction of gender identity. Recent feminist analyses by Third World women have cautioned us against the biases and falsehood of such misrepresentations. For instance, Barbara Omolade has pointed out that African women could participate as human beings with firmly entrenched rights and status in their tribal communities. This position contrasted sharply with their situation under chattel slavery.[10] Similarly, Mary John Mananzan of the Philippines asserts that Philippine women enjoyed a higher status in society before the introduction of Catholicism into their land.[11]

The myths and partial truths of the 'white lady' were maintained as part of an ideology for the domination of the West over other peoples. Western colonialism rested on the assumption of essential differences between the rulers and the ruled. Colonized or subjugated peoples were not treated as equals or subjects, but as 'the other', according to the Korean feminist theologian Chung Hyun Kyung:

> Western colonizers portrayed the Asian as 'the other', not fully 'advanced' like people in the West. Western colonizers did not want to encounter Asians as people by whom they could be challenged, influenced and transformed. Westerners objectified Asians without any willingness to meet and learn from them.[12]

When colonized people were treated as 'the other', their cultural identity and their way of life were not respected or regarded as valuable. White colonizers assumed the supremacy of their own culture, and mission ideology unconsciously provided the religious sanction. Indigenous cultures needed to be transformed to meet the standard of Christian civilization, which was equated simply with white culture. In the name of uplifting their sisters, missionary women played no small part in this cultural transformation. It is often difficult to draw a fine distinction between genuine cultural transmission and ethnocentrism, the more so if the parties involved hold unequal power. On the one hand, white missionary women introduced new conceptions of gender through their work and role model. On the other hand, they were easily tempted to define what was good for other women, and dictate the meaning of feminism in their own terms.

Living under multiple oppression, Third World women saw feminism very differently from the view espoused by evangelical Christianity with its implicit Victorian ideal of womanhood. Many students at mission girls' schools participated in the revolutionary struggles and people's movement at the turn of the century, to the surprise of their missionary teachers. To them, the liberation of women could not be separated from the total liberation from colonialism, economic control and militarism. The rising consciousness of women provided the critical context for them to challenge the patriarchal practices of the church, and the ecclesiologies inherited from the West.[13] Third World women increasingly found the kind of feminism advocated by the white ladies inadequate, because it overlooked the unequal power relations between women.

From the above discussion, it can be seen that the image of the 'white lady' is a social construction which functions to create artificial polarization among women. According to the feminist theorist Trinh T. Minh-ha, identity under conditions of hegemonistic rule is structured so as to keep apart members of different groups by reifying into cultural and social institutions superimposed, mutually irreconcilable essences. At the same time, the uniqueness of other people and the differences shaped by historical and cultural forces are not acknowledged. As a result, the diversity is flattened with no respect for the inviolability of the other's boundaries that delineate our separate identities. According to Trinh:

> Hegemony works at levelling our differences and at standardizing contexts and expectations in the smallest details of our lives. Uncovering this levelling of differences is, therefore, resisting that very notion of difference which, defined in the master's terms, often resorts to the simplicity of essences. Divide and conquer has for centuries been his creed, his formula of success.[14]

The separation of women into different categories prevents them from forming female bonding among themselves. The levelling of differences masks the unarticulated white privileges and power in a colonial situation. Both of these techniques function to serve the political, economic and ecclesial interests of white male supremacy. In order to struggle in solidarity with each other, women must resist the false categorization which places some women on top of others. We have to begin to see our struggles as deeply intertwined and interrelated. Furthermore, we must learn to respect our differences with a recognition that we are each rooted in a separate culture. There is possibility for real dialogue and creative response to this separateness in our co-existence in a multi-cultural and multi-ethnic world.

Notes

1. E. C. Carlson, *The Foochow Missionaries, 1847–1880*, Cambridge, Mass. 1974, 128–9.
2. Mrs A. Bowker and Mrs J. A. Copp, 'To Christian Women, in Behalf of Their Sex in Heathen Lands', *The Missionary Herald* 64, 1868, 139.

3. J. Hunter, *The Gospel of Gentility: American Women Missionaries in Turn-of-the-Century China*, New Haven 1984, 28–9.

4. Ibid., 265.

5. A. H. Tuttle, *Mary Porter Gamewell and Her Story in the Siege of Peking*, New York 1907, 69.

6. Hunter, *Gospel* (n.3), 204–6.

7. Y. J. Allen, *Quandi wu dazhou nüsu tongkao* (Women of all lands), Shanghai 1903, Preface.

8. See P. R. Hill, *The World Their Household: The American Woman's Foreign Movement and Cultural Transformation: 1870–1920*, Ann Arbor 1985.

9. A. R. Drucker, 'The Role of the YWCA in the Development of the Chinese Women's Movement, 1890–1927', *Social Service Review* 53, 1979, 425.

10. B. Omolade, 'Black Women and Feminism', in *The Future of Difference*, ed. H. Eisenstein and A. Jardine, New Brunswick and London 1986, 247–57.

11. M. J. Mananzan, 'The Filipino Women: Before and After the Spanish Conquest of the Philippines', in *Essays on Women*, Manila 1987, 7–36.

12. H. K. Chung, *Struggle to be the Sun Again: Introducing Asian Women's Theology*, Maryknoll and London 1991, 33.

13. P. L. Kwok, 'The Emergence of Asian Feminist Consciousness of Culture and Theology', in *We Dare to Dream*, ed. V. Fabella and S. A. Lee, Maryknoll 1990, 92–100.

14. T. M. H. Trinh, 'Not You/Like You: Post-Colonial Women and the Interlocking Questions of Identity and Difference', *Inscriptions* 3/4, 1988, 72.

Education to Femininity or Education to Feminism?

Mary John Mananzan, OSB

1. Introduction

There is a poster which proclaims, 'Educate a woman and you educate a community'. One can ask, 'Educate her to what?' If this slogan is true, it is indeed puzzling why, after slavery has been declared immoral and revolutions have been fought over class issues, the exploitation and subordination of women still prevails in almost all societies. It is even more appalling to think that women perpetuate their own oppression and that of their daughters and grand-daughters. It is in this context that this article will discuss the socialization of women through education.

2. Main forms of socialization

The most important agents of the ideological apparatus of any society are the family, the educational system, religion and the mass media. They are the most significant means of forming the consciousness of peoples. And though they are distinct systems, they are actually all educational in function, the educational system being institutional and formal while the other three are more informal. These forms of socialization will not receive the same amount of coverage, as this article will concentrate on the more formal form of education.

(i) Socialization in the family

When a baby is born, and when she is put into a pink crib and he is put in a blue crib, the matter is more than an issue of colour. This sets a whole life direction for the new-born baby. Caroline Bird writes:

A small girl learns by the time she is two or three that she is a girl. The nursery books that mother reads her tell what girls are like and what they do. Girls are mommies. Girls are nurses. Mommies care for children. Nurses are helpers. They help men, and doctors are men. The books do not show girl scientists. They do not show sisters leading brothers. They don't show girls making discoveries, creating inventions, making important decisions that others of both sexes follow. Experts tell us children live up to the unspoken expectations of parents. Girls are encouraged to be clean, neat, tender little charmers, while boys are expected to be physically active, exploratory, rebellious and noisy. Boys must be physically competent. They don't have to be talkers.[1]

From the attitude of the adult members of the family and of family friends, the girl somehow absorbs the value that what is important for a girl is to be pretty. Sibling rivalry is seldom caused by envy of the greater intelligence, but by envy of the greater attractiveness of the sibling envied. Girls and women are thus socialized into spending most of their time, energy and money in making themselves physically attractive. The multi-million-dollar beauty industry that depletes the world's natural resources which could otherwise be used for better purposes is based on this brainwashing of women that the most important thing is to be beautiful. This is somehow connected with the idea that a girl has to attract a boy so she can fulfil the highest dream of girls, which is to get married and be wives and mothers. Boys seem to have more self-developmental ambitions in life, like becoming a pilot, a chief surgeon, etc. The formation of a girl, whether it be in deportment, manner of dressing, speaking, attitude, skills, training, etc., is entirely geared to making her valuable in the marriage-market.

Mothers are for ever chiding daughters for being boisterous. Girls are enjoined to be quiet, sweet, pliable, soft, coy, unobtrusive and 'lady-like' – in a word, 'feminine'. They are given dolls, miniature teacups, etc., systematically gearing them to their domestic role. In a Filipino family, sisters are expected to cook for and wash the laundry of their brothers even if these are quite capable of doing this themselves and actually have more time to do such chores. The chores are considered 'women's tasks'. Daughters are usually given home chores while boys may roam about with the excuse that anyway 'boys have no virginity to lose', whereas girls have to be kept busy at home so they are not put into the danger of 'losing their virtue'.

(ii) Socialization in the school
The seed of sex-role stereotyping planted at home is relentlessly pursued

in the school. Sue Sharpe aptly describes what happens:

> School reinforces what children have learnt about sex roles in the family, through the media and in everyday experiences outside the home. Children find for instance that boys and girls are treated differently, boys' activities have higher status than girls' and that boisterous aggressive behaviour is less tolerated for girls. Inside the school these sorts of sex inequalities and differences are perpetuated, together with those of class and race.[2]

Most primary-school teachers are women, and most of them have internalized norms of femininity. They demand obedience, silence, conformity, passivity, all of which are considered characteristics of female behaviour. Girls exhibiting such behaviour gain approval, reinforcing the values learned at home. These are held up as a mark of their greater maturity and responsibility, but as Sue Sharpe laments, 'It is ironic that these same attributes are later used to demonstrate inferiority!' (p. 147).

During this stage, girls are given fairy tales to read. It is alarming how this seemingly wholesome literature inculcates values and attitudes that adversely affect women (the wicked stepmother and step-sisters, the witch, etc.) and the messiah is the Prince Charming, who, when he kisses the heroine, saves her from whatever troubles her, marries her and 'they live happily ever after'.

As the girls go on to high school, the divergence between boys' subjects and girls' subjects becomes wider. Home economics is taught to girls and gardening to boys. Girls somehow get the idea that they are poor in mathematics and good in literature. In fact school timetables are based on the false assumption of what subjects are for boys and what subjects are for girls, without giving them any choice.

It is true that in high school the students no longer read fairy tales, but they go on to Mills and Boon romances which are actually just modern fairy tales with much the same plot and the same values. And because the girls have reached the adolescent stage where sex and romance become a priority, their heads are filled with romantic illusions which they seem never to abandon and which later on they bring to their marriage, thus heading for disillusionment and false expectations. Likewise, the belief that girls find their greatest fulfilment in a husband and children becomes the excuse for their opting out of higher academic pursuits.

When young women get into college their 'feminine values' are fairly entrenched. They find nothing wrong with reading history books written as if no woman ever contributed to history. They are uncritical about literature that portrays women as passive and ineffectual and is written in sexist language. They don't question why there seem to be no great women scientists, artists, musicians. They take courses and major subjects that are expected of women. And they are afraid to complain when they are victims of sexual harassment by male professors. Their domestication is complete – ready to take their role in society as good wives and mothers: the sole responsible partners in making a marriage work or in making a home happy.

(iii) The special influence of religious education

It is amazing how the values of the most secular person who claims to have no religion are actually religious values that have become a part of one's culture and of the collective consciousness of people. Thus many of the sex-role stereotypes that have been discussed have actually come from religious beliefs and principles. Nevertheless, women who have undergone religious education are doubly socialized into the role.

Among the religious teachings that are detrimental to woman are the insistence on her subordination as wife, the identification of her value with virginity if she is unmarried, and the shift of valuation to her reproductive function once she is married. A moral theology based on the dichotomy of body and soul has identified woman with sex and sin and has implanted so much guilt in women that they feel guilty when they are raped; they feel guilty when they are beaten up; they feel guilty when their marriage breaks up; they feel guilty when their children do wrong. The Blessed Virgin who is presented as a model for the woman is often portrayed as a passive and submissive plaster saint instead of the valiant woman in the Bible who sang the strong verses of the Magnificat and stood courageously at the foot of the cross.

The teachings on marriage emphasize woman's secondary and passive role in the family, giving her very little decision regarding her reproductive functions but on the other hand burdening her with almost total responsibility for the good working or the breakdown of the family.

The socialization effected by education and religion is a result of a thousand and one 'little' things which when taken individually may sound petty, but the cumulative effect of which is the successful perpetuation of a patriarchal society.

(iv) The patriarchal paradigm of education to femininity

The above description of the educational process which most women undergo shows very clearly the patriarchal paradigm of mainstream education in most parts of the world, in theory and in practice. Dale Spender analyses the characteristics of this paradigm.[3]

In terms of organization, education is male-defined and controlled, with the result that 'women – and their particular experience of the world – are excluded' (Spender, p. 144). Even if there are more women teachers, still men are the policy-makers in the educational system. It is the men who set the standards and who determine what is significant and relevant, and female experience that does not conform to the yardstick would be considered deviant. Men also predominantly control associations and agencies and periodicals that set the directions of the different educational disciplines. They have also a say in what does and does not get funded as research. The result: 'At every level . . . men are able to exclude women from the construction of knowledge: they can exclude them as subjects when they set up research which is problematic to men, they can exclude them as researchers and theorists by not allocating funding to projects which are perceived as problematic to women and by dis-allowing women's unfunded research . . .' (Spender, p. 147)

The school as an institution is governed by a particular gender regime which may be defined as 'the pattern of practices that constructs various kinds of masculinity and femininity among staff and students, orders them in terms of prestige and power, and constructs a sexual division of labour within the institution'.[4]

Mainstream education, then, is actually *men's studies*. It is deeply entrenched. However, when power is exerted and exerted forcefully, it arouses resistance. In the last ten years, the patriarchal assumptions of the educational system have been questioned and challenged by the feminist movement. Counter-sexist programmes have been started in schools. There is an astounding growth of women's studies courses in many countries. What are the characteristics of this developing feminist model of education? This will be discussed in the next half of this article, both in its general components as well as in the particular experience of a Third World school.

3. Education to feminism

It is difficult to give a finished concept of the feminist model of education, first of all because it is still evolving and because 'it has not been confined to narrow, institutionalized parameters' (Spender, p. 149), but is being developed in varying venues from women's organizations' conscientization seminars to postgraduate courses in universities. However, there are definite trends that are manifested in these various forms.

(i) Trends in the feminist model of education
In the late 1960s, the emerging modern women's liberation movement

started to ask questions about the condition of women. Then, there were no feminist books, no feminist experts, not even adequate data about the situation of women. So there was a need for women to produce this knowledge about themselves. Dale Spender recalls:

> Women found themselves meeting with other women and talking about their personal experience (and validating it in the process); they were constructing a new reality without necessarily being about to state explicitly what it was they were doing . . . None of us (I recollect) had much more than our personal experience to go on. None of us was an expert who could rely on 'book learning'. We were all equal in the sense that we all felt that we had been 'misled and we all wanted to come to understand how it had happened (and to make sure it didn't happen again)'.

This already brings out one trend: the lack of hierarchy in these endeavours and the necessity of co-operative and collaborative methods. Shared knowledge became collective insights which gave rise to new knowledge. And since the starting-point of the process was women's experiences, this knowledge had a direct relation to life and not to abstract theories. The shared experiences also erased the boundaries between teaching and learning. Education became a dialogical process.

There is also an emphasis on the role of the personal which is opposed to patriarchal education. Because of this validation of personal experience, women feel good about themselves after taking women's studies. But women's studies are also political. They aim at empowerment of women, individually and as a group. They question structures: educational and social. They call for structural changes in the educational system, both in theory and in practice, and envision an alternative egalitarian society.

There is also the trend of interdisciplinarity. A. Fitzgerald explains:

> Women's Studies . . . is necessarily interdisciplinary . . . In acknowledging the male-centredness of the traditional curriculum, it points out the biases inherent in all disciplines and thus the political nature of education itself . . . Questioning the underlying assumptions about the truth and supposedly objective knowledge of academic fields is to recognize that the very chopping up and categorizing of knowledge in the academy is itself a political act.[5]

Another feature is creativity in methodology and flexibility. Reacting to the purely rational methodology of mainstream education, feminist education makes use of the arts, performing and visual, in its teaching-learning process. Women perform their reports and do not just read them. In many women's awareness seminars, chairs and tables are pushed aside, and learning happens in very relaxed postures, even some very 'unladylike' ones.

As to the content of feminist education, it includes the analysis of the woman question, gathering data on the issues of women of all sectors, classes, ethnicity, religion, etc. It seeks to find an explanation of the origins of patriarchy and to describe all its manifestations in society. It exposes and neutralizes the forms of socialization that perpetuate the woman question and it outlines an agenda of societal transformation.

(ii) Women's studies, Philippine experience

It is perhaps interesting to trace the evolution of education to femininity to education to feminism by citing a particular case study.

St Scholastica's College is a college for women run by Benedictine Sisters in Manila, Philippines. It was founded in 1906, and although it was first established for the poor, it soon became a school for women of the elite class. As such it aimed at educating women for the traditional roles society had assigned to them. In fact, whatever major subjects the students chose, all had to have Home Arts as their minor.

In 1975, in response to the situation of economic and political injustice in the country, the school was reoriented towards social justice. Its objectives, its curricula, its methodologies and its extra-curricular activities were all geared to create social awareness and to awaken social responsibility and commitment in the academic community.

In the late 1970s and early 1980s, the feminist movement started in the Philippines, and by 1984 a coalition of women's organizations, *Gabriela*, was formed, embracing 105 women's organizations and about 45,000 individual members. Aside from *Gabriela* there were other women's federations. In other words, by then the women's movement was well on its way. But as usual, academe lagged behind.

In 1985, Sr Mary John Mananzan OSB, who was and still is the Dean of St Scholastica's College, was elected national chairperson of *Gabriela*. Seeing how much the women's movement had advanced, it seemed to her appropriate that a women's college like St Scholastica's College should spearhead the establishment of a women's studies programme.

(a) The introductory course to women's studies. In 1985 there were no women with a women's studies degree in the Philippines. This was a blessing in disguise, because the women active in women's organizations were the ones who were recruited to conceptualize the first women's studies course and to teach it. Thus the gap between women's studies

programmes and the programmes of activist women in women's organizations was avoided. Eighteen women committed themselves to pioneer in this new course. In the second semester of 1985, a pilot class was selected, composed of sixteen psychology majors. In the eighteen sessions of the course there were sixteen students and eighteen teachers!

The courses included the following topics: Nature vs Nurture, Physiology of Women, Psychology of Women, Relationships, Images of Women in the Arts and Media, Family and Marriage, Current Issues of Women in the Philippines, Women in Philippine History, Woman and Religion, Patriarchy and Agenda for Renewal.

Because of the enthusiastic response of both students and teachers and the very positive evaluation at the end of the semester, the introductory course was made a part of the general education programme of the college, and therefore a requirement for graduation. In the following year, the Department of Education, Culture and Sports granted the permit for the Cognate on Women's Studies, which consists of twelve units of core studies and six units of electives.

After five years of offering the introductory course, an evaluation of the course was made, using a questionnaire given to all those who were taking the course during the school year 1989–1990. The students once more gave an overwhelmingly positive evaluation, and to the question whether they would recommend the course, most of the students not only said 'yes' but 'most certainly yes', or 'definitely', or 'yes and also to the men', etc.

(b) The establishment of the Institute of Women's Studies. The women's studies programme soon developed other projects besides the curricular one. It was therefore considered advisable to found an Institute of Women's Studies, which received its Securities and Exchange Commission permit to operate in April 1988. Its brochure states the objectives of the Institute:

> to awaken consciousness and provide understanding of the woman question through a formal institutional education strategy;
> to conduct research studies pertaining to gender issues;
> to initiate and administer projects promoting the cause of women;
> to offer outreach programmes for women outside the formal educational institution.

To concretize these objectives, it now offers the following programmes:

1. The research and publication programme

In the assessment of the introductory course on women's studies, one difficulty that surfaced was the lack of local resource materials. The text used was a compilation of readings from the feminist classics written in the

United States and Europe. Although these were very helpful, there was still a need to produce materials which took into account the particular culture and history of the students. This need gave birth to the research and publication programme. The first book written was entitled *Essays on Women*, which was a compilation of the first articles written on women's issues and the women's movement in the Philippines. This is now in a second revised edition. The publication of three more books followed: *Woman and Religion, Women in Arts and Media*, and a book on women in Philippine history written in Filipino.

A new development in this programme is the establishment by seventeen women writers of a women's publishing collective. The women commit themselves to write, translate, illustrate and publish literary books. They have published three books of poems and essays to date. They dream of one day being a women's publishing company.

2. Local outreach

The question arose of extending the course to women who were not enrolled at the college. To answer this perceived need, a module was developed for a three-day awareness-awakening seminar for grass-roots women. Every year, four to six such seminars are given to peasant women, women factory workers, women workers in service industries, and urban poor women.

Another local outreach project focusses on teachers. One insight that has been gained through the years is the need not only to offer a women's studies course but also to develop a women's perspective in all the other disciplines and towards education as a whole. So in collaboration with the Women's Studies Consortium which St Scholastica's College has formed with four other colleges and universities, a module called 'Towards a Gender-Fair Education' was prepared, and seminars and consultations have been undertaken with teachers from the elementary, secondary and tertiary levels as participants. This module consists in analysing the school system and determining sexism in the structure, in the attitudes and in the practices of the schools and the educational materials they use. It then discusses the values of feminist education and provides skill and methods to inculcate these values.

3. Resource development programme

This programme started with the collection of books and audio-visual materials. After some time a considerable amount of material for a vertical file was accumulated. It became clear that there should be a physical centre to house these materials and to open the resource centre to the public.

In 1988, a house and lot beside the school campus was bought for the future centre of the Institute of Women's Studies. The old house was demolished, and in January 1990, the ground-breaking for the new building was held. On 16 December 1990 the three-storey building was finished. It now houses the print and non-print resource centre, the offices of the staff, and dormitory and seminar facilities.

4. The intercultural course on women and society

Requests for training received from women from some countries in Asia and the Pacific prompted the initiation of a three-month course on 'Women and Society' primarily for women of Asia and the Pacific. Its general objective is 'to enable women within the Asia-Pacific region to share, learn and make solidarity linkages with each other in an alternative academic setting'.[6] To date, two such courses have been offered, and the participants have evaluated the course very positively.

4. Conclusion

Feminist education is in its infancy when compared to the entrenched mainstream education, which for women means education to femininity. Helping to perpetuate the ideas and attitudes inculcated by schools is the powerful influence of the media, which are likewise still very sexist and dominated by patriarchal values. Feminist educators are therefore faced with formidable obstacles to their goal of awareness-awakening, empowerment of women and eventually structural changes in institutions and in society.

However, nobody can deny that the feminist movement has made real headway. Many young women today take for granted the freedom they enjoy in different spheres of life, which the feminists of the 1960s fought for. New life-styles and forms of relationships between men and women have emerged. Attitudes have also changed. For example, a study in the United States states: 'While in 1957, 80% felt that an unmarried woman was sick, neurotic, or immoral, two decades later only 25% held that opinion. More than half the populace believes that husbands as well as wives should care for small children; as recently as 1970, just one third thought so.'[7]

And even in feminist education, we read the following optimistic interim assessment (Spender, p. 143):

It can be established that feminism has made great gains within the field of education: the astounding growth of women's studies courses in many countries, the development of alternative and successful models of teaching and learning, the systematic and convincing critiques of the way in which knowledge is constructed and disseminated, and the establishment of diverse and far-reaching research programmes, are all testimony to the feminist achievement within the educational field.

The future is bright!

Notes

1. C. Bird, *Born Females*, Canada 1971, 40–1.

2. S. Sharpe, *Just Like A Girl*, Harmondsworth 1981, 141.

3. D. Spender, 'Education: The Patriarchal Paradigm and the Response to Feminism', in Madeleine Arnot and Gaby Weiner (eds.), *Gender and the Politics of School*, London, 143–53.

4. S. Kessler et al., 'Gender Relations in Secondary Schooling', in Arnot and Weiner (eds.), *Gender and the Politics of School* (n.3), 232.

5. A. Fitzgerald, 'Teaching Interdisciplinary Women's Studies', in *Great Lakes College Association's Faculty Newsletter*, Great Lakes 1978, 3.

6. IWS, *Final Report of the Second Intercultural Course on Women and Society*, 1990, 1.

7. D. Yankelovich, *New Rules*, New York 1981, 58, 93, 94.

II · Feminist Analyses of how Women's Difference is Constructed

The Argument for Women's Difference in Classical Philosophy and Early Christianity

Linda M. Maloney

It should be said at the outset that when the classical Greek philosophers argued for differences between men and women, they (with the partial exception of Plato) were not challenging or attempting to remedy an existing situation. They were simply stating, and rationalizing, the conditions of life in late classical Greece. When Christian writers adopted, or adapted, the same arguments several centuries later, they were engaged in an attempt to reimpose prevailing social norms on sometimes unruly communities, challenged from within by the ideal of a 'discipleship of equals' and from without by those who suspected that Christianity, like other Eastern religions, represented an attack on the institutions of Greco-Roman society. No doubt there were those within the communities, as well, who were made uncomfortable by the overturning of 'normal' patterns of life.

1. Plato

Plato (427–347 BCE) was born into an Athens at war. The Peloponnesian war between Athens and Sparta (431–404 BCE) had led to some relaxation of traditional living patterns, but the climate of Plato's young manhood was one of a city engaged in efforts to restore life as it had been lived in pre-war days. For citizen women, this meant an existence in near-total seclusion. Confined within the parental home until a husband was chosen for her – at which time she would be in her mid-teens, he at least fifteen years older – the Athenian woman of the citizen class would then be transferred to the home of her husband, where she was to fulfil her principal function, of bearing and rearing children. Of those children (on the average, four or five in number, one or two of whom might die at birth), the sons would be raised within the family – particularly in the post-war years when there was a shortage of men – but ordinarily only one daughter, at most, would be reared. Other girl children would probably be exposed; if they did not die, they might be picked up by slave dealers or prostitutes and prepared for a life of slavery, prostitution, or both. Athenian men had a variety of opportunities to satisfy their sexual drive: boys and other men, courtesans or *hetairai*, prostitutes or their own slave women, and wives. The wife's function was, however, primarily that of carrying on the family line and tending the family hearth; sexual satisfaction, for her or her husband, was a marginal issue. The wife did not socialize with her husband and his friends; men's social gatherings, even if held in her own home, were off-limits to her. As for going to the marketplace or communal well, that was an activity reserved for men or for women slaves.[1]

Plato's view of women and men was necessary coloured by the context in which he lived, a society in which the socially-imposed differences between women and men were so obvious that it could be (and was) seriously questioned whether the two sexes shared the same human nature. At times he raised challenges to the status quo; at other moments, his view of the differences between men and women appears to have been thoroughly conventional.

Some of Plato's ideas on humanity may in fact have been derived from the historical Socrates. For example, in the *Meno*, Plato reports Socrates as challenging Gorgias' dictum that virtue differs in men and women. The virtue required for administering a city and the virtue required for running a house are, according to the *Meno*, different in degree, but not in kind. This, in fact, paved the way for the potential equality of the men and women guardians in the *Republic*.[2]

Plato's dialogues contain two proposals for the origin of male and female: the whimsical fable in the *Symposium*, and the more pessimistic account in the *Timaeus*. In the former, Aristophanes recounts how the original humans, who came in three sorts (male, female and hermaphrodite) were separated into halves by Zeus; since then, the halves have been seeking reunion, the formerly male and female entities in homosexual relationships, the former hermaphrodites in male-female relationships. These last are essential for the continuation of the race, but they are also pleasurable for both parties, just as are the homosexual unions.[3]

In the later *Timaeus*, on the other hand, it is only males who are created directly by the gods and are given souls. Those who live rightly return to the stars, but those who are 'cowards or [lead] unrighteous lives may with reason be supposed to have changed into the nature of women in the second generation'.[4] This downward progress may continue through successive reincarnations unless reversed. In this situation, obviously it is only men who are complete human beings and can hope for ultimate fulfilment; the best a woman can hope for is to become a man.[5]

It seems that this ambivalence regarding the innate difference between, and the equal or unequal worth of, women and men is reflected in the two 'utopian' or 'political' dialogues that are closest in time to the *Symposium* and *Timaeus*, namely the *Republic* and *Laws*, respectively. One scholar has suggested that the change in Plato's view of women between the *Symposium/Republic* and *Timaeus/Laws* dialogues can be accounted for by a shift in his attitude towards the physiological theories of Hippocrates, changing from earlier acceptance to later rejection.[6] However, it may simply be that, as Susan Moller Okin believes, the *Republic* represents a model state, which Plato did not hope to see realized, and the second-best city in the *Laws* is more like what he thought could be achieved in fourth-century Greece.[7]

In the *Republic*, Plato makes the startling assertion that, while women as a class must always be inferior to men as a class, they nevertheless possess the same nature and, as individuals, may be equally able to perform the same tasks. He has Socrates assert that some differences affect the pursuits in which people engage; i.e., they constitute qualifications for those pursuits, and others (such as baldness or hairiness in cobblers) do not. And, according to Plato, reproductive roles do not constitute absolute qualifications or disqualifications for governing:

> . . . if the difference consists only in women bearing and men begetting children, this does not amount to a proof that a woman differs from a man in respect of the sort of education she should receive; and we shall therefore continue to maintain that our guardians and their wives ought to have the same pursuits.[8]

This passage hints that for Plato, as Moller Okin points out, 'nature' (*physis*) was not fixed, but was as much the product of education as of birth, perhaps more so. Both the *Republic* and the *Laws* are essentially works of educational theory. Central to the programme for male-female equality in the guardian class of the *Republic* were two changes in the status of things as Plato knew them in Athens: equal education for boys and girls, and the abolition of the family. Before women could become men's equals and carry out equal duties, they had to cease to be the private chattels of their husbands; therefore the abolition of private property among the guardians included the elimination of the chattel status of women. The guardians were to form, in fact, a single 'family' holding all things, including each other, in common, and propagating only as required by the *polis*. They were not even to know which children were their own, that they might cherish them all equally.[9] These arrangements applied, however, only to the guardians; the *status quo* was to be maintained for the lower orders of society.

The essential difference between the *Republic* and the *Laws*, as far as women are concerned, is that in the later dialogue the institution of monogamous marriage is reinstated for all; citizen women, as well as women of the artisan class, are again attached to particular men, and the family is re-established. A necessary corollary is the restriction of women's activities, which once more centre upon the home and allow little time for public service.

In summary, then, the difference between man and woman, for Plato, consisted primarily in their differing reproductive functions, but that difference did not determine the whole of life: given the proper education, and in the absence of lifelong family duties, women were capable, in principle, of filling the same roles as men within their own class.[10] This, at least, is the optimistic view of Plato; the *Timaeus*, on the other hand, seems to assert a 'natural' inferiority of women for which there is no remedy.[11]

2. Aristotle

Plato's student, Aristotle of Stagira (384–322 BCE), had no use for his master's utopian theories. The whole purpose of Aristotle's extensive programme of natural and moral philosophy was the undergirding and reinforcement of things as they are. His notion of scientific knowledge was grounded on the principle that 'what we know is not even capable of being otherwise; of things capable of being otherwise we do not know, when they have passed outside our observation, whether they exist or not. Therefore the object of scientific knowledge is of necessity. Therefore it is eternal . . .'[12] As regards the differences between men and women, then, Aristotle saw it as his task to describe the existing state of things and to explain why it must necessarily be so.

Furthermore, Aristotle's is a functionalist philosophy. Things are defined by their function, and a thing is good or bad in terms of its ability to do what it is supposed to do. 'Function', of course, exists only in relationship; the corollary of Aristotle's functionalism is therefore a hierarchical view of things, in which the 'end' or purpose of the lower is to serve the higher. Not surprisingly, human beings are at the top of the mortal ladder, and the rest of the universe exists for them. But it develops that only men of leisure are 'human beings', in the fullest sense: Aristotle is uncertain about the humanity of slaves; and women, being deficient in the 'deliberative faculty', which makes humans fully human, are also consigned to lower places on the ladder and therefore to the service of the higher. Thus an important distinction appears: males, at least so long as they are members of the leisured class, have the fullness of humanity and are to be served by others; women, whether free or slave, are by definition less than fully human and are destined to serve.

In this area, Aristotle's biological observations were deeply coloured by his vision of things-as-they-are-and-therefore-must-be. His dictum that women are 'defective by nature' is notorious, but it was the consequence of his system. Since it was a fundamental principle for him that, of the two factors or components in every being, 'form' is superior to 'matter', sexual reproduction was considered beneficial, because it demanded that the one who gives the 'form' (the male) be separate from the one who supplies the 'matter' (the female). Thus the 'lower' is not mingled with the 'higher' in the same individual. Aristotle subscribed to what Caroline Whitbeck has called the 'flower pot theory' of human generation.[13] The female, since she is deficient in natural heat, is unable to 'cook' her menstrual fluid to the point of refinement, at which it would become semen (i.e. 'seed'). Therefore her only contribution to the embryo is its matter, and a 'field' in which it can grow. Her inability to produce semen is her deficiency: 'a woman,' Aristotle concludes, 'is as it were an infertile male.'[14] Therefore although Aristotle, like Plato, speaks ambiguously on the question whether male and female are different in their *nature* (*physis*), it is perfectly in accord with his functional view of things to say that, where reproduction is concerned, 'a male is male in virtue of a particular ability, and a female in virtue of a particular inability'.[15]

Since, for Aristotle, a thing is what it is in view of its function, this reproductive situation governs the whole of life: women exist to reproduce human beings; when things go right, they produce men, and when conditions are bad, they produce deficient men, i.e., women. This is a regrettable accident but, in the nature of things, beneficial for the continuation of the race. In his political and ethical teaching, Aristotle developed a consistent code of behaviour for the household which, in contrast to Plato, he regarded as the necessary foundation of society. The free man was the natural ruler of his household, which consisted of wife, children and slaves. Oddly enough, Aristotle blandly notes that 'nature has distinguished between the female and the slave',[16] and sneers at barbarians for failing to make that distinction. Evidently female slaves were completely outside his ken.

In summary, we may say that Aristotle measured women against 'human beings' (i.e., free men) and found them deficient. He defined the differences functionally: women and slaves, each in a different way, existed for the benefit of free men. (He insisted that the benefits were mutual, although certainly the 'higher' member received the greater benefit, and this was as it should be.) Women differ from men precisely by their deficiency: they lack full reproductive capacity, they lack full deliberative power, and they are obviously deficient in physical strength. But they are well suited to be reproductive vehicles and to maintain the family home, the heart of the *polis*, which is the best of all forms of human community.

3. Male and female in the early Christian community

While it is extremely difficult to trace direct lines of influence from the classical Greek philosophers to Christian writers of the first century,[17] we can discern some movements in earliest Christianity whose social ideals were similar to those of Plato at his most radical, and also a series of counter-movements along Aristotelian lines.

The insight that the patriarchal family distorted the capabilities of its members was not unique to Plato. The early Jesus movement in Palestine adopted an anti-familial ethic, calling on Jesus' followers to reject patriarchal family bonds, to abandon house (and the authority exercised or submitted to there), brothers, sisters, mother, father, for the sake of the reign of God. In the 'discipleship of equals'[18] there will again be brothers and sisters, mothers and children, but no fathers. Patriarchy and its central role are overcome. This ethic was to be practised not only by wandering missionaries, but by those at home as well: nothing is said in the earliest traditions about abandoning wives or husbands, but since patriarchy is abolished, the wife-husband roles are transformed into roles of mutual service and even role reversal. The 'last' are now to be 'first' (see Mark 10.29–31 par., as well as Mark 3.31–35; Luke 11.27–28; Mark 10.42–45; Matt. 23.8–11, among others).

A still more explicit rejection of male-female difference based solely on reproductive roles is the pre-Pauline baptismal formula in Gal. 3.28:

For as many as were baptized into Christ have put on Christ.
There is neither Jew nor Greek
There is neither slave nor free

There is no male and female
For you are all one.[19]

Obviously, the elimination of socially-determined 'differences' is the heart of this passage, and the essence of the reality that Christians recognized in the baptismal event. The text clearly modifies Gen. 1.27, in which God created human beings 'male and female'. This passage from Genesis had been used to justify the division of human roles throughout life according to procreative function. The baptismal formula in Gal. 3.28 abolishes that distinction, not by asserting an androgynous humanity, but by reducing the reproductive role to its properly restricted place in human existence. Membership in, and roles of leadership or service in, the Christian community are not determined by gender differences. The Christians who baptized with this formula were in accord with Plato, in the *Republic*, in thinking that procreative capacity was not an appropriate criterion for deciding what functions an individual might perform within the larger community.

This modification of the paradigm of reproductive role as the all-sufficient criterion for determining functions in family and community was explosive in a society dominated by patriarchal convictions that had been elevated to the status of philosophy by the Neopythagorean and Stoic adaptations of Aristotle's thought. Confronted by a church community at Corinth in which women prophets were fully exercising their freedom, and even avoiding marriage in order to preserve that freedom, Paul modified his quotation of the baptismal formula, dropping the 'no male and female' part and emphasizing that 'we were all baptized into one body – Jews or Greeks, slaves or free' (I Cor. 12.13). In another part of the letter, Paul emphasizes the man as image of God, woman as image or 'glory' of the man (I Cor. 11.7–8).[20]

Here, as in the later letters written by Paul's disciples under his name, and in other early Christian correspondence (e.g., I Peter, I Clement), the author's aim is clearly to reverse a trend to the erasing of male-female differences based on reproductive roles. The reasons are equally clear: apart from the individual author's discomfort at the situation, there is the fear of giving offence to the surrounding society. Thus Paul writes: 'Give no offence to Jews or to Greeks or to the church of God, just as I try to please everyone in everything I do' (I Cor. 10.32), and the Pastorals (I and II Timothy and Titus) and I Peter are peppered with exhortations to the Christians not to give offence. Christians lived in a society which agreed with Aristotle that the *status quo* is all there is or should be. Those among the powerful who were discontented with things as they were did not raise their voices in favour of a 'new order'. Rather, they harked longingly back to the 'good old days' of several centuries past, in which life was supposed to have been better because more orderly, with women at the loom and hearth where they belonged. The passion of the author of I Clement is 'order'. In that letter, the supposed golden past of the Corinthian church is portrayed in this way:

> You obeyed your rulers and gave your elders the proper respect . . . You instructed your wives to do everything with a blameless and pure conscience, and to give their husbands the affection they should. You taught them, too, to abide by the rule of obedience and to run their homes with dignity and thorough discretion (I Clement 1.3).

However unrealistic as a portrait of Corinth, this was a state of things that would have won the applause of Aristotle. In such a situation, the desire of Christian men not to be tarred with the calumny of 'seeking to overturn society' was strong. One central means for averting the charge was to show that gender roles within the Christian community were no different from those outside it: that wives submitted to their husbands (I Peter 3.1–6) and lived chaste and sober lives within the house, bearing and rearing children (I Tim. 5.14; Titus 2.4–5).

4. Conclusion

In classical Greece and in Hellenistic society, male-female differences in reproductive roles formed a paradigm by which the 'true essence' of man and woman, and the shape of their lives, was prescribed. For free men, this was a rule of liberation; for women, whether free or slave, it was a rule of subordination and restriction. Any challenge to prescribed social roles for women, therefore, demanded an assault on the family system centred on the reproductive paradigm. But since the male-headed family was the heart of the Greek *polis* and, later, of the Roman civil order, any deviation from the prescribed pattern was viewed with disdain, alarm or outright hostility. Christian challenges to the rigid pattern of male-female relationships were suppressed, sometimes from outside the community, but more often from within. Still, the Gospel writers managed, at the same time, to preserve the 'dangerous memory' of the challenge, founding it on the practice and words of Jesus, and maintaining it as a hope for the future.

Notes

1. See the descriptions of Athenian life in Sarah B. Pomeroy, *Goddesses, Whores, Wives, and Slaves. Women in Classical Antiquity*, New York 1975.

2. Martha Lee Osborne (ed.), *Woman in Western Thought*, New York 1979, 1.2, 'Plato'.

3. See Anne Dickason, 'Anatomy and Destiny: The Role of Biology in Plato's Views of Women', in Carold C. Gould and Marx W. Wartofsky (eds.), *Women and Philosophy. Toward a Theory of Liberation*, New York 1976.

4. Plato, *Timaeus*, 90e. The text of Plato is from *The Dialogues of Plato*, translated by Benjamin Jowett, ed. R. M. Hare and D. A. Russell, London 1970 (4 vols.).

5. Dickason, 'Anatomy and Destiny' (n.3), 49.

6. Hippocrates (460–380BCE), unlike Aristotle, assigns the female an equal biological role in reproduction. See Dickason, 'Anatomy and Destiny' (n.3), 51f.

7. Susan Moller Okin, *Women in Western Political Thought*, Princeton, NJ 1979, Part I: Plato.

8. Plato, *Republic* V, 454e.

9. Moller Okin, *Women in Western Political Thought* (n.7), esp. ch. 2.

10. The intention was not, of course, the emancipation or the good of women: Plato's concern was for the good of the *polis*.

11. For a negative view of Plato see Julia Annas, 'Plato's *Republic* and Feminism', in Osborne (ed.), *Woman in Western Thought* (n.2), 24–33. Annas differs from Dickason (n.3 above) in dating the *Timaeus* at almost the same time as the *Republic*.

12. Aristotle, *Nichomachean Ethics* VI, 1139B. Unless otherwise stated, quotations from Aristotle are from *The Basic Works of Aristotle*, ed. and with an introduction by Richard McKeon, New York 1941.

13. Caroline Whitbeck, 'Theories of Sex Difference', in Gould and Wartofsky (eds.), *Women and Philosophy* (n.3), 54–80.

14. Aristotle, *Generation of Animals* I, 728a, quoted in Moller Okin, *Women in Western Political Thought* (n.7), Part II: Aristotle, 82.

15. Ibid., 82f.

16. Aristotle, *Politics* I, 1252B.

17. See David Balch, *Let Wives be Submissive: The Domestic Code in I Peter*, Atlanta 1981. He traces the influence of the Aristotelian *topos* 'on household management' on the domestic codes in NT letters.

18. See E. Schüssler Fiorenza, *In Memory of Her. A Feminist Theological Reconstruction of Christian Origins*, New York and London 1983.

19. See the text and discussion in ibid., ch. 6, with bibliographic references.

20. See the discussion of all these matters by Antoinette C. Wire, *The Corinthian Women Prophets*, Minneapolis 1990.

The Construction of Women's Difference in the Christian Theological Tradition

Elisabeth Gössmann

The construction of gender difference in the Christian tradition is connected with the reception of the philosophical systems of Platonism, Neoplatonism and Aristotelianism, which were read into the Bible. Though these interpretative syntheses made up of the Bible and Greek philosophy may have had exercised different kinds of influence in particular instances, they were in agreement over the claim that the man was the principal and that the humanity of the woman was derived. To claim that the man was the principal meant that he was the beginning and had a vocation to rule. This presupposition was not questioned either by the church fathers or by most of the representatives of mediaeval Scholasticism. The construct 'woman' was essentially explained as a negation or a reduction of the construct 'man'. Although there are counter-traditions which deviate from this andronormative picture of human beings, right down to modern times (and in both confessions) the main tradition of official theology has proved to be the dominant influence in history because time and again it has been endorsed by the church. The counter-traditions, whether grounded in the plurality of theological schools or conveyed by female mystics or poets, have been put to one side.

Because the same biblical text has continually been interpreted down the centuries, the andronormativeness of the picture of human beings has transcended the bounds of particular periods. Here, apart from some glances back to the patristic period, I shall confine myself to the Middle Ages, with an occasional look forward to the early modern period.

1. Adam, first to be created, the perfect image of God, and the defects of woman. Counter-tradition: Eve, God's masterpiece

Hannah Arendt remarks that action is the only activity of the active life which takes place directly between human beings without the mediation of matter, material and things. The basic condition for action is plurality, 'the fact that not one human being but many human beings live on earth'. According to her, this basic condition becomes clear in the human beings of Genesis 1, created male and female, in the plural. She criticizes the account of the creation in Gen. 2 as follows: 'Here the plural is not original to human beings, but human multiplicity is explained from multiplication. Any idea of human beings, of whatever form, understands human plurality as the result of an infinitely variable reproduction of a primal model.'¹ This applies particularly to the Christian tradition.

The Christian tradition, neglecting the first chapter of Genesis, the significance of which as an independent source (P) it did not yet recognize, concentrated on Genesis 2 (J): all human beings, including women, derive from Adam as the primal model. True, the fact that in Genesis 1 both sexes are in the image of God is not completely suppressed, but in the case of the female sex there are considerably qualifications. According to William of Auxerre (at the beginning of the high scholastic period): 1. the man is directly created in the image of God, but the woman is created only indirectly, through the man (*mediante viro*); 2. the man has a clearer intellect and the woman must be subject to him in accordance with the natural order; 3. all human beings, including women, are to be derived from the one human being, just as all that is created comes from the one God.² This results in the following defect, as far as woman is concerned: she is not the image of God directly, but only through the man – here there was a concern to do justice to I Corinthians 11.7. She is subordinate to the male 'by nature', which makes her dissimilar to God and puts her on the side of creation, since she cannot portray God as Creator in his creativity. So what remains of her *imago Dei*? Scholasticism says that she is not inferior to man in portraying the Trinity through the triad of spiritual powers which Augustine identified (e.g. memory, insight, will). This is not insignificant, since faith and grace begin here and the equality of woman is grounded in redemption. But the consequence of the woman's defect is that she is not called to rule, though this is contrary to Gen. 1.26–28, the charge over creation given to both sexes. Where that is felt to be a contradiction, it is said that the woman forfeited this calling through her role as a seducer in Gen. 3.³

The counter-tradition of women, which can be traced continuously at least from the twelfth to the seventeenth centuries,[4] discovers 'Eve', the last to be created, as the most perfect creature, the radiant image of God and the trace of the divine wisdom. Hildegard of Bingen confirms the male's privilege of physical strength because of his creation from the soil, but accords the woman the privilege of greater skilfulness, subtlety and agility because she is created from human corporeality.[5] Eve's bodily pre-eminence is used apologetically in the women's tradition against the scholastic argument that while the soul is sexless, it can develop its powers better in a male body than in a female body. Women leave aside in eloquent silence the scholastic restrictions on the image of God in women, and stress the image of God in human beings in an egalitarian way, seeking to oppose its distortions. An objection to the denial of similarity to Christ to women is expressed in the saying of Christ that Gertrude the Great receives in a vision: 'As I am the image of God the Father in the Godhead, so you will be the image of my being for humankind.'[6] What the women's tradition reclaimed was the image of God in women, not just as human beings (which was the restriction which Scheeben was still putting on it), but as women. In Marie de Jars de Gournay this is even associated with a disguised demand for ministry in the church;[7] there is also a sign here of the degree to which the concept of the image of God functioned as a forerunner to that of human rights and in this social significance was known to both women and men.

2. Sinful Eve. Counter-tradition: Eve, deceived or indeed innocent

Because (for Catholics at any rate) the interpretation of Genesis 2 which is hostile to women already begins within the Bible, in Sirach 25.24, and is continued in I Timothy 2.13f.,[8] it was almost inevitable for the Christian tradition to project sin and death on to women, a process that also happens in other religions. Granted, church fathers and scholastic theologians attempted to maintain a formal equality of original sin in man and woman by putting more of the burden of original sin on the man in some instances and on the woman in others; however, as the history of the idea demonstrates, it was far more significant that the woman was made primarily responsible for the sin of wanting to be like God. Augustine dismissed the sin of Adam *de facto* as a trivial failing, seeing Adam as having indeed been sinful in disobedience, but making him an accomplice of Eve, who had already incurred guilt, out of sympathy with her, so that she would not be the only one to be lost. In the twelfth century Peter Lombard, on whom all would-be theologians had to comment, speaks of the (cancerous) sore of arrogance in Eve's breast.[9] In the scholastic view, the woman's sin was also made more serious in that she sinned not only against God and against herself, as the man did, but in addition also against her neighbour, by leading him astray into sin.[10]

The identification of the female sex down the centuries with 'Eve, the seductress' provoked a particularly sensitive defence. Whereas Hildegard of Bingen portrayed the first woman as being more deceived by the serpent than sinning and refers to the tumour of pride in the male breast,[11] and Mechthild of Magdeburg stresses the equality of the sin of man and woman, Christine de Pizan begins to acquit Eve. We also sometimes find such an approach among males, but usually in an ambivalent way, as in Henricus Cornelius Agrippa von Nettesheim, in whose work the 'bad Eve' and the 'good Eve' are simply put side by side. However, with women the defence of their own sex in the world in which they live is the motive for the acquittal of Eve, in order to tackle the evil of discrimination at the roots:

> Finally, I must look at the most frivolous arguments of some men. For the most part they argue that Eve was the cause of Adam's sin and consequently of our fall and our misery. My reply is that Eve in no way led Adam to sin, but I believe that she rather simply suggested that he should eat of the forbidden fruit . . . But she did not know that to eat of it was sin, any more than she knew that the serpent . . . was the devil (Lucretia Marinella, 1600).[12]

On the basis of the particular character of Renaissance Platonism, Marinella even succeeded in incorporating the physical and psychological advantages of her own sex into the step-by-step ascent above the beautiful to the divine One, and thus in assigning to the woman the function of being the man's mediator. So this was the opposite of seduction to a 'descent'.

3. The active man and the passive woman. Counter-tradition: the co-operation of the sexes

The claim in Augustine and in Scholasticism that the male intellect has greater clarity is based on biological views from antiquity, derived from natural philosophy and historically obsolete, above all the theory of elements and humours. In the twelfth-century school of Chartres, which was influenced by Platonism, we read that in creating woman God did not mix the elements as well as he did when creating man.[13] The superior elements of the cosmos (fire and air) are identified as 'masculine' and the inferior elements (water and earth) as 'feminine'. From this there results the heat and dryness of the man, which effects a mixture of temperaments more favourable to intellectual development (hence his clearer intellect); the moistness and coldness of the women is the cause of the less favourable mixture of temperaments and consequently of her intellectual weakness. But the activity of the man and the passivity of the woman are also explained in this way: this is a doctrine which becomes increasingly influential, the more Aristotle is accepted without reservations. As a result, with few exceptions, for theologians in the tradition too there is a philosophical explanation for the 'biblical' hierarchy of the sexes, male and female. The harmony of 'Bible' and 'philosophy' proved attractive, and there was no recognition that this was a circular argument.

However, it was not accepted without objections. So already in the twelfth century Hildegard of Bingen developed a cosmic anthropology which broke up the hierarchy of the sexes by pointing to the prominence of the median elements, air and water, in the body of the woman, and of the extreme elements, fire and earth, in the body of the man.[14] Consequently the characteristics of the sexes develop in a polar way; their activities complement each other and each comes to the help of the other. There is an addition to Paul's saying that Eve was created for Adam: as he was created for her.[15] Even if this was long opposed by a legal order determined by androcentrism, here already there are indications of a more or less hidden infiltration of sexual hierarchy.

Strictly speaking, the Franciscan school also took this course, though a first inspection may prove deceptive. Aristotle, who did not understand anything of *sacra scriptura* (= the Bible and salvation history), was not an authority for the Franciscans in this sphere. We notice this at the latest in studying Franciscan Mariology, though at the same time Bonaventure's doctrine of creation also shows a certain proclivity towards a polar image of human beings.[16] The man receives benefits from the woman as she does from him, though the latter is rated higher in the context of the sexual hierarchy of male and female. As the Franciscans did not follow Aristotle, but Hippocrates and Galen, in their biology and psychology of the sexes,[17] they assumed that there was an effective female seed;[18] here they come considerably nearer than the Aristotelian line to the discovery of the female ovum in the 1820s. Actively and passively there is reciprocity between the sexes, even if the activity of the male predominates. So the Franciscans were also interested in a conception of Mary that was free from original sin: like any woman, she too is active in her motherhood, and despite her virginal conception, which prevents the transference of original sin to her child, can nevertheless bequeath her Son a human nature which has been violated and weakened by the consequences of sin, which would disqualify him as redeemer.[18]

This also explains the lack of interest of Thomas Aquinas and his school in the immaculate conception of Mary. There is no question of her handing on any of the consequences of original sin to her son because of the passivity of the woman, to which she is no exception. By contrast, with its objection to the sheer passivity of the woman, the Franciscan tradition overcomes a defect in the female/sex.

4. Woman, disadvantaged by the natural order, natural law and divine law. Counter-tradition: male usurpation

One question often raised in the tradition is whether monogamy is called for by natural law, since the fathers of the faith in the Old Testament evidently did not live in that way. In order to exonerate the Old Testament patriarchs, the answer was that, depending on the requirements of individual periods of history, natural law required at one time that a man should increase his offspring with several wives, or could limit himself to the children of one wife. The latter was regarded as an irreversible rule for the time of the gospel. However, a wife's polyandry was from the beginning and always declared to be an offence against the order or the law of nature: as the Franciscan *Summa Halensis* put it, covering many schools and periods, this was because a woman could not be pregnant by several men at the same time, but several women could bear the children of one man at the same time (*quia una non potest fecundari a pluribus, sed unus bene potest fecundare plures*).[19]

It is illuminating that in the fiction of a woman's polyandry the hierarchy of the sexes is not reversed; the second reason given as to why such a state is contrary to nature is that for many men to be ruled by one woman would not further peace in the family.

Hugo Grotius still thinks just like the Scholastics on this point. Some authors identify marital authority grounded in natural law with that of an absolute ruler. However, Pufendorf limits the polygyny of the man which is possible by natural law by stressing that the marked increase in the number of the population throughout the world has really made it superfluous.

In 1669, Gisbert Voetius of the Reformed Academy at Utrecht held in his *Politica Ecclesiastica* that the greater dignity of man than that of woman was inscribed in the heart of all human beings by the natural law which destines men to rule and women to obey. For him, too, the authority of the father of the house is by divine and natural law. Thomas Aquinas had once, in a Neoplatonic-sounding sentence, described man in his character of ultimate principle within the world and the image of the creator God as origin and goal of woman;[20] Voetius does the same thing, but without citing him. The total withdrawal of the woman behind the man can hardly be expressed more clearly.[21] Of course there was also resistance to this during the transition to the early modern period, when natural-law thinking moved from the sphere of moral theology to that of law. Here we should think not so much of the party with a positive attitude in the struggle for gynaecocracy, since it required women who succeeded to the throne in hereditary monarchies because of the lack of male offspring to give up the feminine ethic of obedient subjection and adopt the male ethic, i.e. as it were undergo a mental change of sex.[22] It is more important to remember the attempt of highborn wives like Marguérite of Navarre, who like many other women, especially in France, wrote an apologia for her own sex. In it she cites the privileged creation of Eve as God's masterpiece as the reason for the political skill of women and roundly declares that the whole of male rule is usurpation.[23] For her the subordination of the woman is the consequence of a male transgression of the law which was noted only by God (Gen. 3.16).

5. Women are to become male. Counter-tradition: We shall encounter Christ in the completeness of our sex (Hildegard of Bingen)

There is a well-known passage in the apocryphal Gospel of Thomas in which Peter seeks to send Mary Magdalene away from the group of disciples on the grounds that women are not worthy of life. The Jesus of this text replies that he will guide her so that she makes herself masculine, so that she becomes a living spirit and thus can enter the kingdom of heaven.[24] It is also well-known that church fathers like Ambrose and Jerome make similar statements: the wife who still serves husband and children and has not yet arrived at full knowledge of faith is called 'woman', but the one who abstains from procreation or is advanced in the faith is called 'man'.[25] Women are enjoined to give up the fleshly and to become spiritual, this being understood as a symbolic (or real?) change of sex, or the possibility is held open for them; here Christianity is by no means alone, but precisely at this point shows parallels with Buddhism (mediated through Gnosticism?).[26]

From the male side, the perfection of a feminine being can be thought of only as 'elevation' and assimilation to the male sex, as a reduction to the one, authentic humanity with a male stamp. So the offer of equality,[27] gladly accepted by those women of Christian antiquity who with male hair-styles and clothing lived as eunuchs in the wilderness or as virgins with their families, was 'Become like us!' In the situation of the time no hostility to women was intended, but the invitation allowed two quite different interpretations: first, the sublation of the feminine (as the imperfect) into the masculine-perfect (as the first and the last); and secondly, the abolition of sexuality altogether, including male sexuality, as a liberation conceived of in Neoplatonic terms. Scotus Eriugena is to be understood in this sense.[28] But the eschatological character of the ascetical movement of late antiquity points to a utopia of sexless human beings.

This is the point at which Augustine tried to direct thought in another direction. Although in his work in particular the positive-negative symbolism of the male and female is presented very strongly where it affects earthly life, Augustine guards against giving up the otherness of the woman as something which would not be worth preserving for the world to come. He resolutely rejects a resurrection of all women as males. As transfigured corporeality has left behind it *libido* and *vitium*, i.e. its weakness conditioned by sin, no conflicts can arise any longer through the female form of humanity, so that Augustine can recognize it in its creaturely beauty: 'To be a woman is no vice, but is natural.'[29] This had to be said at all because of the mood of the culture of late antiquity into which Christianity was born, and to which it had assimilated itself in its interpretation of the Bible.

With his doctrine of the preservation of womanhood in the eschaton, Augustine gave the Middle Ages a good dowry. This gift also proved useful in the fight against dualistic sects which still spoke of women (eschatologically) becoming men. Mediaeval women who write and who stress their womanhood as *virgines* – though also showing signs of solidarity with the *matres* – leave the symbols of becoming male behind them and combine their theme of feminine modesty, with which they introduce their works, with a strong consciousness of election.

I hope that it has become clear from this much abbreviated account that despite the tenacity of the androcentric, patriarchal tradition, some modifications were possible to its construct 'woman'. For want of relevant research we cannot determine clearly to what extent counter-traditions were the occasion for this. However, the fact that the counter-traditions had to struggle for centuries in attempts to refute the same prejudices against the female sex indicates their lack of success.

If the impression has arisen that the doctrines of the counter-traditions were mere reversals, i.e. over-valuations of feminine humanity which had been previously been undervalued, the answer must be that this is not the case. For the counter-traditions are concerned with a 'negation of negation'.[30] The construct of a femininity which has not attained complete humanity, defined in andronormative terms, is rejected: the starting point is that of the originality of woman's being and an attempt to describe this not as derived, but as independent humanity. Meditating on texts like this can help present-day women and men to get past thinking in terms of a single principle and develop that dual (not dualistic nor even just polar) model of humankind which we still lack.

Translated by John Bowden

Notes

1. Hannah Arendt, *Vita activa oder vom tätigen Leben*, Stuttgart 1960, 15f.
2. William of Auxerre, *Summa Aurea*, ed. Pigouchet (Paris 1500), Frankfurt am Main 1964, fol. 58v.
3. Ian Maclean, *The Renaissance Notion of Women*, Cambridge 1980.
4. Cf. my article 'Eva, Gottebenbildlichkeit und Spiritualität', in *Wörterbuch der Feministischen Theologie*, Gütersloh 1991.
5. Elisabeth Gössmann, '*Ipsa enim quasi domus sapientiae*. Zur frauenbezogenen Spiritualität Hildegards von Bingen', in Margot Schmidt and Dieter R. Bauer (eds.), '*Eine Höhe über die nichts geht.' Spezielle Glaubenserfahrung in der Frauenmystik?*, Stuttgart and Bad Cannstadt 1986, 1–18, esp. 9–11.
6. Gertrude the Great, *Legatus divinae pietatis*, translated by Johanna Lanczkowski, Heidelberg 1989, 25.
7. There is an introduction to Marie de Jars de Gournay in Elisabeth Gössmann (ed.), *Archiv für philosophie- und theologiegeschichtliche Frauenforschung*, Vol. 1, Munich 1984, Ch. 1, cf. esp. 28f.
8. Cf. Helen Schüngel-Straumann, *Die Frau am Anfang. Eva und die Folgen*, Freiburg 1989.
9. For Augustine and Peter Lombard see the relevant chapters in Monika Leisch-Kiesl, *Eva in Kunst und Theologie des Frühchristentums und Mittelalters. Zur Bedeutung 'Evas' für die Anthropologie der Frau*, Theological Dissertation, Salzburg 1990.
10. For this theme see also the chapter, 'Der Mensch als Mann und Frau', in my Habilitation thesis, *Metaphysik und Heilsgeschichte. Eine theologische Untersuchung der Summa Halensis*, Munich 1964, 215–29, and my 'Anthropologie und soziale Stellung der Frau nach Summen und Sentenzenkommentaren des 13. Jahrhunderts', *Miscellanea Mediaevalia* 12.1, Berlin 1979, 281–97.
11. Cf. Barbara J. Newman, *O feminea forma. God and Woman in the Works of St Hildegard*, PhD dissertation, Yale University 1981.
12. There is an introduction to Lucretia Marinella in Elisabeth Gössman (ed.), *Archiv für Philosophie- und theologiegeschichtliche Frauenforschung* 2, Munich 1985, Chapter 1; the quotation is on p. 41. For Henricus Cornelius Agrippa von Nettesheim, cf. Vol. 5 of the same archive (Munich 1988), introductions and text.
13. Cf. Hans Liebeschütz, *Kosmologische Motive in der Frühscholastik. Vorträge der Bibliothek Warburg 1923–24*, ed. F. Saxl, Leipzig and Berlin 1926, esp.128.

14. Cf. Prudence Allen, *The Concept of Woman. The Aristotelian Revolution*, Montreal and London 1985; id., 'Two Medieval Views on Woman's Identity: Hildegard of Bingen and Thomas Aquinas', *Studies in Religion. A Canadian Journal* 16, 1987, 21–36.

15. *Scivias* I.2, Migne, PL 197, 393; CCM 43, 21.

16. Cf. my attempt to investigate the connection between system and the image of woman among the Franciscans in Theodor Schneider (ed.), *Mann und Frau – Grundproblem theologischer Anthropologie*, Freiburg 1989, 44–52.

17. Cf. Emma Therese Healy, *Woman according to St Bonaventure*, Erie, Pennsylvania 1965, 11f. Albertus Magnus also assumed that the seed in woman was inactive. Cf. Paul Hossfeld, 'Albertus Magnus über die Frau', *Trierer Theologische Zeitschrift* 91, 1982, 221–40.

18. Cf. Elisabeth Gössmann and Dieter R. Bauer (eds.), *Maria für alle Frauen oder über allen Frauen?*, Freiburg 1989, 63–85.

19. *Summa Fratris Alexandri*, Tom. IV L.III, Quaracchi 1948, nos. 253–5.

20. Thomas Aquinas, *Summa Theologia* I q 93 a. 4 ad 1; *'Nam vir est principium mulieris et finis, sicut Deus est principium et finis totius creaturae.'*

21. *Politicae Ecclesiasticae Pars II*, Amsterdam 1669, Liber I Tr. 4, *De mulieribus*, p. 186: *'Vir est origo et principium ex quo mulier, et est finis propter quem producta est mulier.'*

22. Cf. Maclean, *Renaissance Notion* (n.3), 62f.

23. For Marguérite of Navarre, cf. *Archiv* (n.7), 13f.

24. For the Gospel of Thomas and its cultural environment see Peter Brown, *The Body and Society. Men, Women and Sexual Renunciation in Early Christianity*, New York and London 1988, esp. 113, with further literature.

25. A long time ago attention was already drawn to these texts and connections by Haye van der Meer, *Priestertum der Frau? Eine theologiegeschichtliche Untersuchung*, Freiburg 1969. For Jerome and Ambrose see 97f.

26. Cf. Elisabeth Gössmann, 'Haruko Okano, Himmel ohne Frauen? Zur Eschatologie des weiblichen Menschseins in östlicher und westlicher Religion', in *Das Gold im Wachs, Festschrift für Thomas Immoos*, ed. E. Gössmann and G. Zobel, Munich 1988, 397–426.

27. Cf. Ruth Albrecht, *Das Leben des hl.Makrina auf dem Hintergrund der Thekla-Traditionen*, Göttingen 1986; Kari Vogt, 'Becoming Male. One Aspect of an Early Christian Anthropology', *Concilium* 182, 1985, 72–83.

28. For Scotus Eriugena cf. the works by Werner Beierwaltes, esp. *Denken des Einen. Studien zur neuplatonischen Philosophie und ihrer Wirkungsgeschichte*, Frankfurt am Main 1985.

29. *'Non est autem vitium sexus femineus, sed natura'*, *De civitate Dei* 22.17, 18.

30. The formula comes from Katharina Fietze, *Spiegel der Vernunft. Theorien zum Menschsein der Frau in der Anthropologie des 15. Jahrhunderts*, Munich philosophical dissertation 1990 (planned publication Paderborn 1991).

Gender and Moral Precepts in Ancient Mexico: Sahagun's Texts

Sylvia Marcos

'Daughter, my beloved, my dear little dove . . . these words are . . . precious like fine well-cut gems. Take them and keep them in your heart, write them deep within you . . .'

(Aztec *huehuetlatolli* as recorded by Sahagun)

Wisdom from the ancestors, from the 'female ancestors, the noble ladies, old and grey-haired, the grandmothers', from the 'elders, wise and prudent men and women' (Sahagun 1989) is contained in the highly polished formulations of the ancient Aztec *huehuetlatolli*. Part of a long, rich oral tradition, they include precepts and sayings that describe expected behaviour and adult responsibilities. In written form they appear in Book VI of the *Florentine Codex* by Fray Bernardino de Sahagun, a Franciscan missionary who arrived shortly after the conquest of Mexico. As moral precepts, they are a key to the interplay between culture and behaviour.

Recent feminist scholarship in Mexico suggests that these texts confirm the passive and submissive feminine role in Aztec society. That reading may appear valid if only the precepts for girls are considered (L. Arizpe 1984, G. Hierro 1990, M. Rodriguez 1989). However, analysing all the precepts – those directed at boys as well as those for girls – reveals an underlying ideology of gender balance.

There are indications that within Mesoamerican societies women participated in political life in significant ways. In a previous work (Marcos 1976), I discuss these instances and their sources. For example, in the *Anales de Cuautitlan*, it is recorded that six women and six men were elected to rule collectively. In areas under Aztec rule, the custom of calling one of two governing elders *'Cihuacoatl'* or 'Snake Woman' indicates the value given the feminine element (Sahagun 1989). Women also owned property and at times led warriors in battle. In the *Selden Codex* there is a reference to a warrior princess who defended her domain. Hernan Cortes in his *Five Letters to the Emperor* tells of a local woman ruler who blocked the advance of the Spaniards on their march to Tenochtitlan.

The 500th anniversary in 1992 of the 'encounter' of two worlds provides an opportunity to discuss some of the values and traditions of the new world peoples which were overshadowed, lost or transformed in that process. Their cosmology formed the basis for their way of being in the world.

Mesoamerican cosmology was based on the idea of dualities and opposites and the search for balance. Duality appeared in every religious duty, political activity and domestic task. The starting point for my study of gender construction is this key element of the Mesoamerican world-view: the duality of complementary opposites as discussed by all major Mesoamerican scholars (see Alfredo Lopez Austin and Miguel Leon-Portilla). My concern, then, is to analyse how this characteristic is both at the root of gender and shapes gender in Mesoamerican societies.

Feminist theoreticians have affirmed the 'inseparability of gender and other social relations . . . (A)s a result, we can no longer assume a universal determinate of the social construction of gender' (Malson et al. 1989). By focussing on the intersection between gender and moral precepts, this article will attempt to provide insight into a cultural arrangement that does not seem to foster or validate rigid and mutually exclusive gender categories.

Reviewing the highly polished formulations concerning proper conduct in ancient Mexico contained in the *huehuetlatolli* will hopefully serve to broaden the ongoing discussion concerning socially constructed gender behaviour.

Duality in Nahuatl cosmology

Religious and social aspects of pre-Columbian society were tightly interwoven: religion, philosophy, the arts, war, agriculture and social relations formed a whole which reflected the dominant world view or cosmovision. Aztecs[1] regarded their deities as the suprapersonal unity that made the collective more important than the sum of its members. Of the Aztec god of war, *Huitzilopochtli*, Sahagun's native informants said, 'he is but subject and prince', meaning, 'he is no more than the people as a whole, from the highest to the lowest' (Sahagun 1989).

References to Nahuatl goddesses and gods in Sahagun's texts reveal a complex concept of divinity. The Aztecs generally used the word *teotl* (literally 'stony' but figuratively 'permanent' or 'powerful') for their deities

(Parrinder 1984). They attributed various qualities to them, but one characteristic that most deities shared was a dual nature, a mixture of feminine and masculine traits in varying degrees (Marcos 1989a). Both genders fused, for example, in Coatlicue, the serpent-skirted Aztec goddess (Fernandez 1959). Tlaloc, the rain deity, had no specifically female or male traits as pictured in the Tepantitla mural of Teotihuacan (Nash/Leacock 1982). In Tlazolteotl, the deity associated with birth and 'that which is cast off' (Karttunen 1988), feminine and masculine attributes merged (Sahagun 1988; Heyden 1977).

Many ancient Mesoamerican deities were goddess-god pairs beginning with the supreme creator, Ometeotl, whose name means 'two-god' or 'double god'. Inhabiting the highest upper world, the thirteenth heaven, Ometeotl was thought of as a feminine and masculine pair. Other deities, descendants of the supreme pair, were in their turn natural phenomena.

Duality in the Mesoamerican cosmovision was not fixed and static, but fluid and constantly changing. This was a key element in Nahua thought. Deities, people, plants, animals, space, time and the cardinal directions all had a sexual identity as female or male, and this identity shifted constantly along a continuum. Gender permeated every aspect of life as an ever-changing identity. The primordial dualism in Mesoamerica was dynamic, and this mixed female and male valence manifested in religion and everyday life (Gossen 1986).

Balance was important as a sustaining force in the universe and in society, as will be seen in the following exploration of gender and its relation to cosmology. Opposing forces or apparently opposite ends of a polarity must be kept in balance in the universe, in society and in the individual. Awareness of balance and the need to restore it was (and is) the basis for Mesoamerican healing practices (Lopez Austin 1971, Viesca 1984, Marcos 1988). Within the four levels of earth where the Nahuas lived (their universe had nine underworlds and thirteen upper worlds), there was nothing that was exclusively female or male. Within this realm, all beings combined gender characteristics in varying degrees (Lopez Austin 1990). Feminine and masculine attributes merged into fluid entities. These expressed the shifting equilibrium of opposite forces which in their turn reflected the fundamental balance of the cosmos and society. From the individual to the cosmic, gender appeared as the root metaphor of balance.

This highly esteemed ideal of equilibrium was recommended as a pattern of conduct for the young adults of the community. Other examples of duality are found in nature and in the social structure. Many have an implicit gender component.

Life and death as no more than two aspects of the same reality are expressed in the pottery of Tlatilco with two faces, one life-like and the other representing a skull. The sun and the moon were seen as combinations of the feminine and masculine (Baez-Jorge 1988). When newborns were purified by ritual bathing, feminine and masculine waters were invoked (Sahagun 1969, 1989). Likewise corn could be feminine (*Xilonen-Chicomecoatl*) and masculine (*Cinteotl-Itzlacoliuhqui*).

Even the Mesoamerican calendar was dual: the ritual calendar consisted of thirteen cycles of twenty days each; the solar calendar had eighteen twenty-day cycles and a five-day period to correct the calendar. Speech and poetry likewise reflected doubleness: important statements were repeated in pairs with minimal changes (Garibay 1964, Sullivan 1983). Much Nahuatl poetry is made up of pairs of verses in which the order may vary, but the two members of the pair may not be separated. Among other researchers, Lopez Austin (1988) perceives the whole of Mesoamerican thought in terms of duality.

Mesoamerican deities, like everything in the cosmos, had two complementary parts: female and male, beneficent and malevolent, light and dark, etc. 'What we might perceive as a disturbing contradiction, the Mesoamericans from their point of view see as complementarity, wholeness and harmony' (Karttunen 1986). But these are not static dichotomies. Gender identities moved along a shifting continuum where the determining factor was the attainment and maintenance of balance. In the *huehuetlatolli* we can see these basic principles of Nahua thought in the context of daily life and social relations.

Sahagun's dilemma

The written forms of the elders' orations on behaviour date from the period after the conquest. Although for the most part the military battles had ended, the era was marked by Spain's attempt to consolidate its control over the original inhabitants of Mesoamerica and was filled with the tension of conflicts between two sharply divergent world-views and social organizations. Bloody battles had left a relatively small group of colonizers in political control. The beautiful Aztec city of Tenochtitlan was destroyed, the imposing temples were burned and the awesome statues of the goddesses and gods smashed. Native populations, now subdued, came under the influence of missionaries such as 'The Twelve' – a dozen Franciscan friars who arrived in 1525 with great enthusiasm to convert the Indians to Christianity (Ricard 1982). In 1529 another group of missionaries arrived, and among them was Fray Bernardino de Sahagun. The seeming compliance of the Indians led the evangelizers to believe that conversion was being accomplished easily and quickly.

However, after the efforts of the first years, the friars of New Spain noted that far from truly converting the Indians (Klor de Alva et al. 1988), their work had laid the basis for the emergence of a new configuration of religious elements. Despite the efforts of the missionaries, in most cases they simply provided the native population with another set of sacred personages and rituals that were worked into the existing structure in an original way (Burkhart 1989).[2] Now the missionaries were no longer so sure of their effectiveness. They realized that much of the supposedly vanquished culture had escaped their control and that Christianization was inadvertently fostering practices and ceremonies in the churches that kept alive what ecclesiastical authorities termed 'idolatries'.

Fray Bernardino de Sahagun, who had already demonstrated interest in the people being catechized and had translated the Bible into Nahuatl, was ordered to write an extensive manual about native beliefs and practices. Sahagun understood that to convert the Indians successfully would require profound knowledge of their customs, values, beliefs and language.[3] Beginning in 1547 and using his ample knowledge of the main indigenous language, he compiled prayers, songs, admonitory discourses and other examples of highly polished, metaphorical and literary expression from the formal oral tradition. Thus, when he was asked in 1558 to record in Nahuatl what would be useful for catechizers to know about the people they were teaching, he used the opportunity to describe the old culture and its ways. He spent years interviewing the elders of two towns near the capital, Tepepulco and Tlatelolco. From long conversations and questionnaires and with the aid of Indian assistants, he gathered material for his 'ethnographic encyclopedia', as Burkhart (1989) calls it. But Sahagun's systematic presentation of the important elements of Nahua belief and ritual, medical practices, religious festivities, hymns to deities and other forms of expression raised the suspicion that he was spreading 'idolatries'. The Franciscan friar had to face persecution by church authorities and his Nahuatl texts were not translated into Spanish until 1575.

His keen perception and rigorous investigation gave rich detail to his *General History of the Things of New Spain* or the *Florentine Codex*. Alfredo Lopez Austin states, 'The bilingual work which records to the letter the responses of the elder informants constitutes the greatest source for the study of the ancient Nahuas' (Sahagun 1989). According to Klor de Alva, the text is 'the fullest record available of the natives' own reconstruction of their culture' (1989). Pictographic material provided by

Indian scribes accompanies the Nahuatl and Spanish versions and was the basis for parts of the written text.

Although Sahagun's purpose was to help in the conversion of the Indians, he was also sincerely interested in them and their culture, and aligned himself with those who fought to protect them. Thus he was anxious to emphasize the similarities between native religious practices and moral codes and his Spanish Catholic values. This explains why, although his text contains numerous references to women, it underplays their position in Aztec society. Researchers who have investigated this discrepancy include B. A. Brown (1983) and A. Ichon (1973).[4] Finally, Nash comments that the accompanying pictographs indicate greater participation by women than is observable in the text (1978).

The *Florentine Codex* has, of course, been analysed from several viewpoints by many scholars (Lopez Austin 1988, Leon Portilla 1988, Gibbson 1964, Klor de Alva et al. 1988), and there is almost no scholar of ancient Mexico who has not based the major part of his or her research on this or a similar basic text. Concerning issues of gender, however, even though some studies have emphasized the abundant presence of women (Hellbom 1967, Rodriguez 1988), the implications of this presence for issues of complementarity and of duality in relation to gender have been researched by only a few scholars (Nash 1978, Nash and Leacock 1982).

Ancient moral precepts

Through its focus on social precepts, Book Six of the Florentine Codex reveals Nahua values. The texts contain the ethical teachings embodied in formal discourses known as *huehuetlatolli*, or the 'precepts of the elders'. Elders were referred to as ritual ancestors, as descendants of the founders of the Aztec lineage. The older women and men of Mesoamerican communities were repositories of wisdom and knowledge; they could acquire prestige and were often regarded as having great vital energy. Consequently, they merited respect and were considered very powerful (Lopez Austin 1988, Sahagun 1969).

The *huehuetlatolli* that survived the conquest were transcribed by both native speakers and missionaries in the Spanish-based alphabet worked out for Nahuatl.[5] *Huehuetlatolli* include parental orations as well as discourses for religious occasions. Merchants, artisans and healers and other professions had their orations. Other orations related to life-cycle events. The midwife's words to a mother on the birth of her child are a striking and well-known example of a life-cycle discourse. A woman giving birth was regarded as a warrior going into battle. In the orations before birth, the midwife urged her to fight her battle bravely. When the child was born, the midwife would give a war cry meaning that

> . . . the woman had fought her battle well . . . she had taken a captive, she had captured a child (Sahagun 1969).

The importance of the *huehuetlatolli* for the Nahuas is summed up by Thelma Sullivan:

> Every important event in the life of an Aztec . . . was punctuated by long, eloquent orations appropriate to the occasion. It was in the rhythmic phrases of these orations with their exquisite metaphors, complementary phrases, and carefully selected synonyms, that the religious, moral, social, and political concepts of the Aztec were transmitted from generation to generation. The *huehuetlatolli* were the great repositories of Aztec traditions and wisdom, and in the corpus of Aztec literature they stand out as the most revealing of the Aztec mind and thought (Sullivan 1986).

Among those who have contributed to the literature on the *huehuetlatolli* are Baudot (1979), who analyses their literary structure, and Karttunen and Lockhart (1987), who look at them from a linguistic and literary point of view. The orations have been studied for the wealth of cultural information that they reveal (Leon-Portilla 1988). Lopez Austin (1984) refers to them as 'Mexica-education' and Thelma Sullivan gave her study of the orations a Nahua metaphor as its title: *A Scattering of Jades: The Words of the Aztec Elders* (1986).

The *huehuetlatolli* presented below were addressed to daughters and sons at the appropriate moment when they began to show signs of physical maturity. These texts have often been quoted in a piecemeal fashion, citing only the advice for young girls because it appears to reinforce rigid gender roles familiar to Western researchers (Brumfiel 1990). Texts are seldom balanced with references to the advice given to young men. However, once the precepts are compared, they reveal much cultural material concerning gender and show the gender-bound behaviour expected of both young women and men in Ancient Mexico as well as providing the basis for understanding some key elements of Aztec thought.

Voices of the elders

'. . . My beloved daughter, my little dove . . . precious as a gold bead and a rare feather . . . listen attentively to what I have to say . . .' (Sahagun 1989, p. 365).

'. . . My dearly cherished one, you are my son . . . precious gem . . .
beautiful feathers . . . I have decided to tell you some things owing to
my duty as your father . . .' (p. 373).

Expressions of affection, flowery speech and use of metaphor often
appeared in the first part of the discourses for both young women and men.
Aztecs were concerned about the proper way to enjoy the pleasures of
life. Some of the orations include phrases like:

'Daughter, . . . our Lord gave us laughter and sleep, eating and
drinking with which we sustain ourselves. God also gave us the craft of
begetting by which we multiply in the world. All these things provide
some contentment in our lives for a little while . . .' (p. 366)

Life is pleasurable by the Lord's command; pleasure was regarded as a
gift to be enjoyed and savoured.

'My son . . . the world has this way of generating and increasing, and for
this begetting, God ordered that a woman require a man, and a man a
woman . . .' (p. 381).

As Lopez Austin notes (1988), sexuality was considered a pleasure given
by God to alleviate pain on earth. But Fray Bernardino de Sahagun,
struggling to present the Indians in a way acceptable to the church, muted
this divine command. It was transformed into *'el oficio de la generacion'*
(literally, the craft of generation). While pleasures in life should be
regarded as a gift from God, nothing exempted the Nahua from a concern
with balance:

'Daughter . . . Do not throw yourself into the fetid dung of lust . . .'
(p. 369);

'Son . . . Do not throw yourself at a woman like a dog throws itself on its
food . . .' (p. 381).

Daughters were advised not to look men over as if they were 'fresh cobs
of corn, to find the best and tastiest' (p. 369).
Because of Sahagun's interest in helping the Indians, he stressed
similarities between their values and Spanish Catholic values and played
down the divergences. But occasionally despite his best attempts,
metaphors such as the one above strongly hint at a different attitude
towards pleasure.

Seldom do ancient texts give such a clear, detailed and homely presentation of ethical norms in a society as do these Nahua texts, which recommend the most noble and admired forms of conduct in all areas of adult life for young people just entering adulthood.

But truly to penetrate these moral recommendations, we must place them in the specific context of Aztec beliefs formed by cosmology and experience. For the Nahua peoples of Mesoamerica, conduct was not a matter of individual expression. Human behaviour was a life-and-death matter. As Burkhart notes, 'The Nahuas had no concept of punishment for sins after death, but they did believe that human acts could provoke a final cataclysm' (1989). The fear of bringing upon themselves chaos and destruction through their personal behaviour operated within the larger framework of collective responsibility (Wolf 1959). Breaking the norms had effects that went beyond the individual and altered the cosmic order itself. Thus an individual who erred was a danger to the survival of the collective, and elimination of the disturbance had to be rigorous, radical and immediate in order to mitigate the threat to the cosmos. Instead of a concept of personal moral goodness and self-righteous behaviour, the Nahuas believed that a connection existed between individual failings and the effects of this failure, not only for the individual but for the entire community.[7] Collective responsibility had another side, however, since it implied the possibility of creating and sustaining the universe. Existence demanded discipline of the Nahuas, but also implied power.

Even these limited selections from the *huehuetlatolli* demonstrate that although the precepts were directed to the sexes separately, there is no implication that one sex is superior to the other. Fulfilment of duties is presented as essential to proper living, and correct conduct is insisted upon for sons as well as daughters. For example, both young women and young men were expected to fulfil their religious obligations:

'Daughter, . . . Do not be overly fond of sleep. You should rise up in the night, sweep,[8] wash the mouths of the gods and offer them incense . . .' (p. 367).

'My son, . . . the first thing is that you be very mindful to waken and maintain vigil without sleeping all the night . . . You must rise at night . . . And take care to sweep the place where the images stand and offer them incense' (p. 383).

Hard work was expected from both sexes, but each had a domain of production. Weaving was an important productive activity that women carried out. Not only did their weaving supply clothing, but it also produced wealth. Lengths of woven cloth or 'mantas' were used as exchange for the purchase of many products and for the payment of tribute (Garibay 1965). Young girls were encouraged to strive for mastery and excellence as weavers. Boys were told to plant corn, fruit and agave. The productive activities of women and men complemented each other: one sex's activity was not regarded as more valuable than that of the other.

'Daughter . . . learn well how to make food and drink . . . learn soon how to make chocolate . . . or grind corn or how to weave and embroider . . .' (p. 367).

'Son, be watchful that you sow the cornfields, that you plant magueys and tunas (cactus fruit) and fruit trees . . .' (p. 364).

Aztec society, after its first great victories in the central plateau, evolved into a militaristic society that valued, above all, war-related activities from which women were generally excluded. However, women had a domain in which by performing their tasks well they attained the same esteem accorded the courageous warrior:

'And if you are adept at your tasks . . . you will be praised and honoured . . . and you will value yourself as if you were in the ranks of those who merit honour for their feats in war. You will merit the eagle standard like good soldiers. And if by chance you are adroit in your crafts like a soldier in battle . . .' (p. 368).

Honour as warriors was also given, as mentioned above, to women when they gave birth and brought back 'a captive'; those who died in childbirth were likewise honoured as fallen warriors.

These examples are of advice for each sex that is equivalent. Below are examples of conduct recommendations for such mundane activities as dressing, eating and walking that are similar for girls and boys . . .

'Daughter, . . . do not walk hurriedly nor slowly . . . because walking slowly is a sign of pompousness and walking quickly reveals restlessness and little sense. Walk moderately . . . Do not walk with your head lowered or your body slouched, but also do not carry your head overly high and upright because this is a sign of bad upbringing' (p. 371).

'Son . . . take care when you go about the streets or roadways that you walk calmly, neither in a great hurry nor too slowly, but with forthrightness and measure . . . Do not go about head down, nor stooped over, head to one side, nor looking every which way, so that they say you are . . . badly brought up and undisciplined . . .' (p. 383).

Balance in dress was recommended; the expectations for both sexes were similar:

'Daughter, . . . Do not dress yourself with curious and elaborate things because this signifies extravagance . . . Nor is it appropriate that your garments be ugly, or dirty or torn . . .' (p. 370–1).

'Son, . . . your garments (should) be modest and unadorned. Do not dress strangely, nor extravagantly, nor eccentrically' (p. 384).

The counsels for marriage relations, however, were different for young women and men. Women were counselled to have only one sexual partner:

'. . . When God wills you to take a husband, . . . look, do not give licence to your heart to be drawn somewhere else . . . at no time and nowhere should you commit the betrayal called adultery, . . . look, do not give your body to another' (p. 372).

Boys did not have this restriction, but they were warned about the danger of becoming like 'dried maguey' and being useless to their women:

'You will be like the maguey whose sap is dried up . . . and whoever tries to get nectar from you gets nothing . . .' (p. 381).

'. . . Your wife, because you are dried up and no good any more and have nothing to give her, will reject you because you do not satisfy her desire, and she will look for another because you are worn out. And even though she has not the intention to do it, because of your lack she will commit adultery' (p. 382).[9]

In the *huehuetlatolli* men are portrayed as in danger of 'drying up' and needing to conserve their forces, but women did not have this problem. In one of the discourses for young men, we find a story that illustrates a difference in perception of the sexes. Two older women, grandmothers with 'white hair, wiry like sisal fibre' were discovered having sexual relations with two young temple attendants and were brought before lord Netzahualcoyotzin. This excerpt has been cited often (Quezada 1973, Baudot 1973). But its implication for gender issues has not been elaborated (Marcos 1989b).

Lord Netzahualcoyotzin, apparently surprised by these old women who were still active and interested in pleasure, asked them,

'Grandmothers, tell me, is it true that you are still interested in pleasures of the flesh . . . being as old as you are?'

The old women replied with a long explanation that ended with a metaphor:

'. . . (W)e women never tire of these doings nor do we get enough because our bodies are like a deep abyss that never fills up; it takes in everything, wanting and demanding more and more . . .' (p. 382–3).[10]

Besides complementary recommendations for behaviour in marriage, both were told eroticism was a gift from the Lord, but they were expected to manage it wisely. Both were expected not to be too passionate, to be able to wait for the ritual moments in the Aztec calendar of festivities when it was indulged. Again the ideal of balance appears. Sexuality also had religious connotations. Ritual sexuality in the temples has been recorded along with ritual abstinence (Sahagun 1988). What was absolutely rejected was the fixation of behaviour at one of the extremes. For example, absolute repression of sexuality was considered abnormal.

In another article I have analysed erotic poetry and data that seem to reveal erotic elements in the culture (Marcos 1989b), but it is also true that discipline was important. The opposites were always present; two seemingly distinct poles fused. Opposites show themselves to be complementary.

This ideal of balance was an essential element of Nahua thought. To find and maintain it was a constant concern, and required finding the centre of the cosmos and one's position in relation to that centre. To maintain equilibrium was to balance opposites. This was done not by negating the extremes, but by acknowledging and embracing them and finding that ever-shifting point of equilibrium. In the Nahua universe, nothing was negated: good and evil, hot and cold, life and death, night and day, upper world and lower world, feminine and masculine.

Conclusion

The texts of the precepts passed on to the young members of the community seem to reflect a society where the construction of gender was based on the idea of balance and acceptance of duality and its necessary opposites. The *huehuetlatolli* we have just reviewed reveal a social construction of gender within Aztec morality where similarity and/or equivalence appear as the norm for the community rather than gender hierarchy or superiority. The equilibrium that was so valued in the society served as both the measure and expression of individual and collective well-being. Absence of balance implied the threat of disturbance in the cosmos.

Gender was the abiding metaphor that sustained, constructed and explained the cosmos. Gender oppositions, as well as other oppositions in the Mesoamerican universe, shared the common characteristic of all dualities: the imperative to transcend the extremes. Women and men reproduced in themselves a reflection of the equilibrium essential to Mesoamerican cosmology.

Edited and translated by Jacqueline Mosio

Notes

1. Aztecs (also called 'Mexicas') were only one of the Nahua speakers. Nahua is a much broader category geographically and temporally. Mesoamerican is an even broader geographical and cultural area which includes the Nahuas and many other language groups. I will use the terms interchangeably in this article.

2. Immediately after the conquest and Christianization, the indigenous population openly followed their long-established pattern of assimilation and integration of the new religious figures and beliefs into existing structures. The friars interpreted this acceptance of Christianity within their own cultural and theological context.

3. Not until 1537 in the Papal Bull *Sublime Deus* did Pope Paul III decree that the inhabitants of the new world were human beings.

4. This theme is discussed eloquently by Irene Silverblatt in relation to primary historical sources in Peru (1987).

5. The inhabitants of Mesoamerica had developed a pictographic writing system and they recorded events, commerce and ritual by means of descriptive paintings in bark paper books. This co-existed with and depended on a strong oral tradition which survives in some forms today. Contemporary ethnographers report instances from Indian villages of advice still being passed on in formal rhetorical, poetic discourses (Karttunen 1986, Good 1990). However, the scope of this discussion does not permit their inclusion.

6. The *huehuetlatolli* texts used in this article are taken from the Spanish version of the *Florentine Codex* with paleography, introduction and notes by Alfredo Lopez Austin and Josefina Garcia Quintana. Another missionary, Fray Andrew de Olmos, began collecting *huehuetlatolli* in 1533 and incorporated some of them in his *Gramatica de la lengua Mexicana* originally published in 1547.

7. We can contrast this moral ethos with that of the third-century Romans discussed by Foucault in *The Care of the Self* in *History of Sexuality*, vol. III. For the Romans, 'balance' and 'harmony' refer to *inner* virtues cultivated for *individual* self-development. This is in sharp contrast to the Nahua idea of collective responsibility which was the basis of both the concept of sacrifice and the celebration of erotic pleasure.

8. Sweeping was not merely the act of cleaning. It had the ritual and metaphorical meaning of opening the way for the gods to enter (Soustelle 1961).

9. These texts could indicate that adultery on the part of women was expected and fairly common.

10. Is Sahagun reading his European Catholic formation into this incident and shifting from a Nahuatl concept to a concept of his own concerning the sexual nature of

women? Compare the idea of women's sexual 'insatiability' found in *Malleus Malificarum*.

I wish to thank Alredo Lopez Austin, Rosalind Petchesky, June Nash and Hal Benenson for their helpful critical comments on this article.

Research for this article was made possible by a Rockefeller Humanist in Residence Grant at the Hunter College Women's Studies Program. Special thanks to its director, Rosalind Petchesky, and to the many colleagues and students who provided support and stimulus for my work.

Bibliography

Baez-Jorge, F., *Los Oficios de las diosas*, Universidad Veracruzana, Xalapa 1988

Baudot, G., *Las letras precolombinas*, Siglo Veintiuno, Mexico 1979 (*Les Lettres Précolombiennes*, 1976)

Brown, B. A., 'Seen but not Heard: Women in Aztec Ritual – The Sahagun Texts', in *Art and Image in Pre-Columbian Art*, ed. J. C. Berlo, Oxford 1983

Brumfiel, E., 'Weaving and Cooking: Women's Production in Aztec Mexico', in *Women and Pre-History*, ed. J. Gero and M. Conkey, Oxford 1990

Burkhart, L. M., *The Slippery Earth*, Tucson, Arizona 1989

Fernandez, J., *Coatlicue: Estetica del arte indigena Antiquo*, Universidad Nacional Autonoma de Mexico, Mexico 1959

Garibay, A., *La Literatura de los Aztecas*, Mexico 1964

—— (ed.), 'Historia de los Mexicanos por sus pinturas', in *Teogonia e historia de los Mexicanos. Tres opusculos del siglo XVI*, Mexico 1965

Gibbson, C., *The Aztecs Under Spanish Rule*, Stanford 1964

Good, C., personal communication, 1990

Hellbom, A., *La participacion cultural de las mujeres indias y mestizas en el Mexico precortesiano y pos-revolucionario*, The Ethnographical Museum, Stockholm 1967

Heyden, D., *El aspecto androgino de los dioses mexicanos del post-clasico tardio*, Lecture given in Guanajuato, Mexico, Deasinah 1977

Ichon, A., *La religion de los Totonacos de la Sierra*, Instituto Nacional Indigenista, Mexico 1973

Karttunen, F., 'The Survival of Indigenous Social Organization and Values in Mesoamerica', Lecture delivered at the Institute for Development Studies, Helsinki 1986

Karttunen, F., and J. Lockhart, *The Art of Nahuatl Speech: The Bancroft Dialogues*, UCLA Latin American Center, Los Angeles 1987

Klor de Alva, J., H. B. Nicholson and E. Q. Keber, *The Work of Bernardino de Sahagun*, Albany, New York 1988

Klor de Alva, J., 'European Spirit and Mesoamerican Matter: Sahagun and the "Crisis of Representation" in Sixteenth-Century Ethnography', in *The Imagination of Matter* (ed.), David Carrasco, Bar International Series, Oxford 1989

Leon-Portilla, M., *Huehuetlatolli: Testimonios de la antiqua palabra*, Facsimile reproduction and introduction, Comision Nacional Conmemorativa del V Centenario del Encuentro de Dos Mundos, Instituto de Investigaciones Antropologicas, Mexico 1988

——, *Toltecayotl, aspectos de la cultura nahuatl*, Fondo de Cultura Economica, Mexico 1980

Lopez Austin, A., *The Human Body and Ideology* (1980), Vols. I and II, Salt Lake City 1988

——, *La educacion entre los Mexicas*, Universidad Nacional Autonoma de Mexico, Mexico 1984

——, Lecture given in Mexico City at Deas-Inah 1990

Malson, M., et al., *Feminist Theory in Practice and Process*, Chicago 1989

Marcos, S., 'La mujer en la Sociedad Prehispanica', in *La mujer en Mexico: Epoca Prehispanica*, Departamento del Distrito Federal, Mexico 1976

——, 'Mujeres, Cosmovision y Medicina: Las Curanderas Mexicanas', *Trabajo, poder y sexualidad*, El Colegio de Mexico, Mexico 1989a

——, 'Curas, Diosas y Eroticismo: el Catolicismo frente a los Indios', in *Mujeres e Eglesia: sexualidad y aborto en America Latina*, Catholics for Free Choice-Fontamara, Washington-Mexico 1989b

Nash, J., 'The Aztecs and the Ideology of Male Dominance', *Signs. Journal of Women in Culture and Society*, 1978, 4.2

Nash, J., and E. Leacock, 'Ideologies of Sex: Archetypes and Stereotypes', in *Cross-Cultural Research at Issue*, ed. L. Leob Adler, New York 1982

Nicholson, H. B., *Religions in Pre-Hispanic Central Mexico*, Handbook of Middle American Indians, Vol. 10, *Archeology of Northern Mesoamerica*, Part I, ed. R. Wanchope, G. F. Ekholm, I. Bernal, Austin, Texas 1971

Parrinder, G., 'Aztecs and Mayas', *World Religions from Ancient History to the Present*, New York 1984

Quezada, N., *Amor y magia amorosa entre los Aztecas*, Universidad Nacional Autonoma de Mexico, Mexico 1973

Ricard, T., *The Spiritual Conquest of Mexico* (1933), Berkeley 1982

Rodriguez, M. J., *La Mujer Azteca*, Universidad Autonoma del Estado de Mexico, Toluca 1988

Sahagun, Fray Bernardino de, *Historia General de las Cosas de Nueva Espana*, Tomo I, Introduction, paleography, etc., ed. A. Lopez Austin and J. Garcia Quintana, Mexico 1989

——, *Florentine Codex: General History of the Things of New Spain*, trans. of original Nahuatl text by A. Anderson and C. Dibble, Salt Lake City 1969

Silverblatt, I., *Moon, Sun, and Witches: Gender Ideologies and Class in Inca and Colonial Peru*, Princeton 1987

Soustelle, J., *Daily Life of the Aztecs* (1955), Stanford 1961

Sullivan, T., *Compendio de la gramatica Nahuatl*, Universidad Nacional Autonoma de Mexico, Mexico 1983

——, 'A Scattering of Jades: The Words of the Aztec Elders', in Gossen, G., *Symbol and Meaning Beyond the Closed Community: Essays in Mesoamerican Ideas*, Institute for Mesoamerican Studies, Albany 1986

Wolf, E., *Sons of the Shaking Earth*, Chicago 1959

Viesca, C., 'Prevencion y Terapeuticas Mexicas', in *Historia General de la medicina en Mexico*, Book I, ed. A. Lopez Austin and C. Viesca, Mexico 1984

Gender and Knowledge in Western Philosophy: The 'Man of Reason' and the 'Feminine' 'Other' in Enlightenment and Romantic Thought

Sarah Coakley

In much recent Western theology,[1] and more especially in feminist philosophy and theology,[2] an anti-hero stalks: the Enlightenment 'Man of Reason'. Can we not all agree in despising him? This villain has a number of characteristics. Cogitating, lonely, individualist, despising of the body, passions, women and indeed all sociality, he artificially abstracts from the very dependencies he takes for granted: the products of earth, the comforts of family and friends, and – not least – the miraculous appearance of regular meals.

But like many stereotypes, this 'Man of Reason' is himself an amalgam, a police identikit constructed from a variety of witnesses. In what follows I shall attempt to interrogate at least a few of the more influential amongst these Enlightenment witnesses, and to range their views alongside Romanticism's (ostensibly compensatory) quest for divine mediation through the 'eternal feminine'. My paradoxical conclusion, to anticipate, is that whilst the view of 'women' to emerge from these authors is on the whole depressingly unanimous in its stereotypes,[3] the various views of 'man' that they promulgate are not ones which modern feminists can afford to reject *simpliciter*. At the very least, or so I shall argue, they present us with remaining 'antinomies' with which feminism, and especially Christian feminism, is still struggling.

'Man of Reason'

Consider, first, the relation between 'man' and 'nature' as construed by Francis Bacon (1561–1626). Genevieve Lloyd rightly draws attention to the distinctively 'modern' tone of Bacon's argument: rejecting the classical Platonic quest for 'ideal forms' adumbrated in the natural world, Bacon construes matter as straightforwardly mechanistic; the task of the (male) scientific 'mind' is to attend to the mechanism, to experiment and test until predictive control is achieved. Notoriously, Bacon then identifies 'Nature' here as 'female', urging the scientist to enter a 'holy and legal wedlock', to 'bind [Nature] to your service and make her your slave'.[4] Despite Bacon's (touching?) request for 'chastity' and 'respect' in this 'marriage', the gender lines have been fatally drawn. And yet here is also our first enduring paradox for current feminism: for whereas some contemporary feminists (especially historians and anthropologists) are busy deconstructing, or relativizing, the view of 'nature' as a universal datum at all (let alone a datum identified with the 'female'),[5] other, 'radical', feminists rejoice in Bacon's very identification of 'nature' and 'women', urging instead a new release of the 'roaring inside her'.[6]

If we associate Bacon's witness with 'male' control of a 'female' Nature, René Descartes (1596–1650) is more commonly charged with creating a different, but arguably even more fatal, dualism between mind and body. In his famous *Second Meditation* Descartes conducts a thought-experiment of abstraction from the body until he arrives at a notion of identity distinct from it: 'At last I have discovered it – thought – this alone is inseparable from me.' But Descartes' views on the mind/body relation are more subtle and complex than he is commonly given credit for (and arguably the nature of their connection is never fully clarified).[7] But what Descartes strongly denies (in the *Sixth Meditation*) is any suggestion that his mind is in his body 'only as a pilot in a vessel'. And in his late work, *The Passions of the Soul*, he insists that 'the soul is united to all the portions of the body conjointly', speculating (curiously, as it now seems to us) that the bodily seat of the soul is not 'the whole of the brain' but the pineal gland.

It is as well to remember, too, the theistic moorings of Descartes' *cogito*, his underscoring of the significance of the radical *dependence* of the soul upon God, and his religious motivation in asserting its distinction from the body – its immortality. On a secular reading, Descartes' dualism may look crass and insupportable; but for Christians (including Christian feminists) it is hard to see how at least a *distinction* between soul and body – which is not the same as an ultimate separation – can be avoided. Again, then, we have remaining paradoxes here: we may well criticize the way Descartes has construed the soul/body relation, but it is hard to dispose of the problem altogether. Descartes' thinking was not explicitly sexist: in principle, the exercise of Reason was as open to women as to men, but, as emerges revealingly in his correspondence with the Princess Elizabeth, the arduous demands of his particular form of abstract reasoning were hard for a woman to sustain: 'Sometimes the interests of my household,' complains Elizabeth, 'sometimes conversations and civilities I cannot eschew . . . [do not] allow me enough free time to acquire a habit of meditation in accordance with your rules.'[8] From this perspective we may see the emergence of feminist epistemologies (such as Sara Ruddick's[9]) as a fit rejoinder to Descartes: the emphasis here is not so much on soul/body dualism as on the sheer complexity of maternal decision-making in the maelstrom of toddlers' demands and emotional blackmail. In this way we may turn Descartes (justly!) on his head, and defend the high sophistication of 'maternal thinking', the forging of peace and harmony and nurture out of the confused interstices of domestic existence.

If Descartes leaves a more complex intellectual inheritance for feminism than is often allowed, the legacy of Jean-Jacques Rousseau (1712–78) is even more bewildering, indeed riddled with self-contradictions.[10] Exponent of vegetarianism and maternal breast-feeding, he himself fathered five illegitimate children who were left as foundlings; protected and sustained at crucial points in his career by rich and dedicated women, he himself recommended that the education of girls should merely attune them to lives of subordination ('Unable to judge for themselves, they should accept the judgment of father and husband . . .' *Émile*, Bk. V); devoting *The Social Contract* to an acute analysis of why 'man [*sic*] is born free' but yet 'everywhere . . . is in chains', he granted women no such ambitions to liberty and equality.

And yet Rousseau was an adulator of women, a positive defender of the importance of the family, the body, feeling and the imagination, as emerges especially from *Émile*, and from his novel *La Nouvelle Héloïse*.[11] Here is no clear case, then, of our identikit 'Man of Reason'. Rather than rending thought and body apart, Rousseau constructed a rather different series of aligned dualities (male/female, reason/nature, reason/passion, public/private), based on a theory of sexual difference and 'complementarity'. Women are held up as close to Nature, as moral exemplars, as potentially dangerous in their capacity for passion, but as safely containable within the private, domestic enclave. (Julie, in *La Nouvelle Héloïse*, manifests all these traits: she cultivates a little garden in which 'Nature has done everything'; she early falls prey to passion in the loss of her virginity to her tutor Saint-Preux, but places duty to her family before this passion, submitting to an appropriate marriage and domestic 'happiness', whilst yet finding real happiness elusive.[12]) On the other side of the sexual divide, 'male' Reason emerges dynamically from Nature ('The passage from the state of nature to the civil state produces a very remarkable change in man, by substituting justice for instinct . . .', *Social Contract* I, ch. VIII); yet there is also nostalgia for the 'natural' state, and a hope that the transformation of society might effect a new *rapprochement*. Reason, however, must hold sway in the public realm, lest passionate feelings conflict with the demands of state order.

It will be clear, perhaps, that Rousseau's theory of sexual 'complementarity' actually presents a 'difference' between the sexes by no means predicated on equality (and this point was not lost on Mary Wollstonecraft, Rousseau's spirited assailant on this issue in *The Vindication of the Rights of Women*, 1792). Thus, in *Émile* we are told that, 'A perfect man and a perfect woman should no more be alike in mind than in face . . . In the union of the sexes, each alike contributes to the common end, but in *different* ways.' Reading on, the sting in the tail becomes apparent: 'From this diversity springs the first difference which may be observed between man and woman in their moral relations. The man should be strong and active; the woman should be weak and passive; the one must have both the power and the will; it is enough that the other should offer little resistance.'[13] No wonder, perhaps, that both Rousseau's famous heroines, Sophie in *Émile* (who loses her virtue decisively when she moves to a 'public', urban domain), and Julie in *La Nouvelle Héloïse* (who maintains a listless virtue in marriage), have to be killed off at the end of their stories: their *subordinate* 'complementarity' leaves them little room for manoeuvre.

The remaining paradoxes of Rousseau's thought, then, are differently located from Descartes': the rhetoric of 'difference' still continues to fascinate (especially in contemporary French feminism), and indeed must do, if we are to avoid a straightforward aping of a 'masculinist' vision of humanity. Yet 'liberal feminism' (witness Mary Wollstonecraft herself) is understandably suspicious of any version of sexual 'complementarity' dreamed up by men; Enlightenment ideals of freedom, equality and autonomy might seem preferable in comparison. This gender tension is, interestingly, transferred and *internalized* in Rousseau in what Margaret Canovan has described as his 'longing for autonomy (to the point of solitude), on the one hand, and for integration (to the point of self-annihilation) on the other'.[14] Falling in love is a dangerous (albeit necessary) business in Rousseau's writings: *dependency* is, according to him, both an enticing requirement of sexual love and also its destructive pathology. Is there no way through this dilemma?[15]

The answer of Immanuel Kant (1724–1804), of course, was that autonomous reason should transcend any entanglements of dependency or 'heteronomy'. In this way he shuns Rousseau's fascination with sexual love and feeling. His essay 'What is Enlightenment?' (1784) is a charter document of independent critical judgment: '*Sapere aude*' (Dare to be wise) means the sloughing off of immature submission to mere authority; the individual must dare to take responsibility for entry into the public realm of universal principles of reason and morality. Significantly, Kant underscores that the 'entire fair sex' avoids this 'step to competence'. Yet ostensibly, the Kantian autonomous individual is sexless. Indeed in the *Groundwork for a Metaphysic of Morals* (1785), for instance, Kant insists that the moral principles enunciated there are not only applicable to all human beings, but to 'rational beings' *per se*. Sex seems irrelevant; especially when, in the *Critique of Pure Reason* ([1]1781, [2]1787), the strange 'noumenal self' 'independent of, and free for all . . . necessity' is contrasted with the 'phenomenal self', known through actions in the empirical world. What, then, are we to make of the rampant sexisms of Kant's political writings, and especially his discussion 'Of the Nature of the Sexes' in the *Anthropology*? Here, as Susan Mendus puts it, 'Kant's mind, almost wholly uncluttered by any actual experience, is laid bare and the prejudice and bigotry are revealed.'[16] A married woman, for instance, is represented as promiscuous and unreliable, jealous and harsh ('In marriage the husband loves only his one wife, but the wife has an inclination for all men', etc.); no justification is given for these assertions, but the conclusion, notoriously, is that 'the woman should reign and the man should rule; because inclination reigns and reason rules.' The domestic power of women is ultimately superseded. No wonder, then, that in Kant's political philosophy women are only accorded the status of *passive* citizens; and in marriage woman is seen as relinquishing her equality in deference to 'the natural superiority of the husband over the wife'.

As Mendus concludes, 'It may well be that Kant is an honest but narrow-minded bourgeois, unable to see beyond the social conventions of his time.' But are his sexisms merely incidental? The more interesting question is whether his distinctive view of the autonomous, independent dispassionate *individual* 'cannot readily accommodate . . . social units such as the family, which transcend mere atomism',[17] and hence make the construction of this view of the self parasitic upon the submission of women (and indeed man-servants). It is, then, the paradox of 'autonomy' and 'heteronomy' that Kant's form of the 'Man of Reason' abidingly bequeathes to modern feminism. If women claim a Kantian form of autonomy, they risk all the traps of atomism; but if they compromise it, they fall back into subordination, or perhaps never fully emerge from the soup of undifferentiated relationship.

The 'eternal feminine' of Romanticism

Romanticism's answer to this problem was to compensate for the lonely male 'autonomy' by an adulation, indeed near deification, of the 'feminine'. Once again, we are not dealing with a consensus of views; the earlier writings of Friedrich von Schlegel (1772–1829), in particular, could have a surprisingly 'modern' ring, viciously lampooning the emotive sex stereotyping of Schiller's lilting rhymes ('The Husband must enter/The hostile life/With struggle and strife. . . . [but] Within sits Another/the Chaste Housewife/The mild one, the mother – /Her home is her life').[18] Briefly, in the early Schlegel is an alternative vision (focussed on the model of Antigone, but probably inspired by a real-life woman, Caroline Böhmer) of an independent woman achieving completion without the benefits of male love.[19] Much more characteristic of Romanticism, however, was an aspiration to 'androgyny' achieved through the love union; and to this view Schlegel himself later subscribed.

Sara Friedrichsmeyer[20] has recently traced the sources of the Romantics' *Androgyne* ideal. It goes back at least to Plato's *Symposium*, and Aristophanes' story there of the split selves who roam about in search of each other; but the Romantics' reassimilation of the theme was part of their fascination with esoteric literature – especially alchemy – and with their background in German pietist thought, itself influenced by the Protestant mystic Jakob Böhme. In all these sources the myth of the androgyne appears in some form; in Böhme (censored till 1682) there are daring justifications for sexual desire as a 'divine inclination', and Christ's last words on the cross (*consummatum est*) are taken to signify some final merging of the sexes.

In the Romantics, the myth can collect a number of different evocations. In Novalis's novels, 'romanticizing the world' means raising the 'lower self' to 'an elevated meaning . . . [of] an infinite lustre'; thus (male) consciousness is raised by contact with female inspiration, and the symbol of the androgyne represents their union. The working out of this theme, especially in Heinrich von Ofterdingen, is, as Marilyn Massey has demonstrated,[21] sexually and politically daring, even outrageous: it combines an unbridled eroticism, and (amongst other things) an adulation of unmarried goddess-mothers, and strange rites such as the drinking of the dissolved ashes of a mother so that she can be 'present in each'. The sexually arousing is (not unusually) combined with the fantasy world of the weird and wonderful. But it is revealing to know that Novalis's real-life experience of androgynous union was the idealization of a twelve-year-old girl, Sophie, whom he met and fell in love with; she died three years later, but Novalis claimed to have some experience of mystic union with her (and with the world of spirit) at her graveside. Sophie's extreme youthfulness and her premature death are surely significant, and invite guesses both about the maturity of the androgynous relationship envisaged and about the extent of the woman's reciprocity in it. Is she ultimately dispensable?

The fate of Gretchen in Goethe's *Faust* is no less revealing of a double standard: for while Gretchen is responsible for the high task (as *das ewig Weibliche*) of leading Faust's soul to eternal salvation, she must herself nonetheless do penance for her own sexual transgression. 'Perhaps,' comment Susan Cocalis and Kay Goodman, 'it is this inequity that constitutes the real tragedy of Goethe's *Faust*.'[22] Likewise, it is hardly reassuring to be told (by Wilhelm von Humboldt) that women are 'closer' to the ideal human than men, when it turns out that any kind of active self-assertion or manifest talent is frowned upon in their case as 'unfeminine'.[23] The serious inequalities and sexisms of 'androgyny', balanced in favour of *male* development and integration, are manifest here, and notoriously repeat themselves in C. G. Jung's theory of the self some generations later, where the incorporation of a woman's *animus* is treated much more summarily (and indeed negatively) than the integration of a man's ('feminine') *anima*.

In Schlegel's novel *Lucinde*, in contrast, the lovers Julius and Lucinde exchange roles in their love-making (Julius exhibiting 'charming surrender', Lucinde 'considerate ardour'), and in this androgynous exchange Julius finds a 'wonderful . . . allegory of the development of male and female to full and complete humanity'. Despite the shift, then, from his earlier phase to the more obviously Romantic interpretation of the 'androgynous' idea, we see here in Schlegel a slightly more equitable interpretation of the theme. Arguably too, in Schleiermacher's 'Christmas Eve Dialogue' we have expressions of religious 'feeling' and the 'feminine soul' just as well represented by Josef (who chides the other men for their tedious speech-making and himself 'laughs and exults like a child') as by Sophie, the little girl who more obviously exhibits the spirit of Christmas and spontaneous religiosity.[24]

We may well conclude: all Romantic 'androgynes' are 'equal', but some are decidedly more equal than others. But again, the paradoxes of this Romantic theme have far from been dispelled: the obsession with sexual 'difference' is still with us, and the idea (in radical feminists such as Adrienne Rich) that female nature, and motherhood, are capable of producing new and distinctive 'visions' of the world ironically echoes Romantic forebears. And when we recall that early Romanticism wished to loose men and women from fixed concepts of gender (whilst not retreating into an abstract sexless account of the person), we realize that that agenda is still with us too, however poorly it was served by individual Romantics' solutions. Moreover, for Christian feminism especially, the huge question still remains (poignantly begged by Romanticism) of the integration of sexual desire and the desire for God, and the extent to which such an integration might be constructed out of the resources of Christian history and spirituality. Is falling in love invariably nothing but a false delusion, a pathology of sexual dependence? Or is it in some way capable of alignment with a feminist account of human growth before God?[25]

Conclusions

By a selective (and necessarily brief) account of Enlightenment and Romantic visions of the normative male self, and by reference to some of the burgeoning feminist literature on this topic, I have sought to avoid some of the more simplistic stereotypes of this 'Man of Reason' and to urge that many of the issues raised by the thinkers concerned are still – paradoxically – pressing ones for contemporary feminist thought. In short, our Enlightenment heritage is not easily dispelled; indeed without it, it is hard to imagine modern Western feminism having taken the form it has in the first place. And as the heady shift to post-modern relativism becomes an attractive philosophical option for increasing numbers of feminists, we may well question whether the Enlightenment demand for global principles in ethics (as opposed to *local* political agendas) can be lightly discarded when what we surely must still dream of is an 'abolition of the sex class system' *tout court*.[26]

Notes

1. See especially F. Kerr, *Theology after Wittgenstein*, Oxford 1986, ch. 1.

2. See especially G. Lloyd, *Man of Reason*, London 1984; S. M. Okin, *Women in Western Political Thought*, London 1980; E. Kennedy and S. Mendus (eds.), *Women in Western Political Philosophy*, Brighton 1987; and consider the influence on feminist theology of C. Gilligan, *In a Different Voice*, Cambridge, Mass. 1982.

3. See Kennedy and Mendus, *Women in Western Political Philosophy* (n.2), 16ff., for a résumé of the pervasive stereotypes of emotionality and submissiveness.

4. Lloyd, *Man of Reason* (n.2), 12, citing Bacon's *The Masculine Birth of Time* (1653).

5. See e.g., C. P. MacCormack and M. Strathern (eds.), *Nature, Culture and Gender*, Cambridge 1980.

6. See S. Griffin, *Women and Nature: The Roaring Inside Her*, London 1984.

7. So A. Kenny, *Descartes*, New York 1968, 222–3.

8. Lloyd, *Man of Reason* (n.2), 48–9, citing a letter of Princess Elizabeth to Descartes, 10/20 June 1643.

9. S. Ruddick, *Maternal Thinking*, Boston 1989.

10. There is now an extensive feminist literature on Rousseau. As well as Lloyd, *Man of Reason* (n.2); Okin, *Women in Western Political Thought* (n.2); Kennedy and Mendus, *Women in Western Political Philosophy* (n.2), see also J. B. Elshtain, *Meditations on Modern Political Thought*, New York 1986, and J. B. Elshtain (ed.), *The Family in Political Thought*, Brighton 1982.

11. For discussion of these aspects of Rousseau's thought see especially Elshtain, *Meditations* (n.10), ch. 4.

12. See Okin, *Women* (n.2), ch. 8, for a treatment of this.

13. For discussion of this see C. W. Korsmeyer, 'Reason and Morals in the Early Feminist Movement: Mary Wollstonecraft', in C. G. Gould and M. W. Wartofsky (eds.), *Women and Philosophy*, New York 1976, 97–111, especially 99.

14. In Kennedy and Mendus, *Women* (n.2), 79.

15. See the discussion of this question in E. Rapaport, 'On the Future of Love: Rousseau and the Radical Feminists', in Gould and Wartofsky, *Women and Philosophy* (n.13), 185–205.

16. See Kennedy and Mendus, *Women* (n.2), 35.

17. Ibid., 40f.

18. Ibid., 106–7.

19. See the discussion in S. Friedrichsmeyer, *The Androgyne in Early German Romanticism*, Bern 1983, ch. 5.

20. Ibid., chs. 1, 2.

21. M. Massey, *Feminine Soul: The Fate of an Ideal*, Boston 1985.

22. S. L. Cocalis and K. Goodman (eds.), *Beyond the Eternal Feminine*, Stuttgart 1982.

23. Kennedy and Mendus, *Women* (n.2), 110–11.

24. So D. de Vries, 'Schleiermacher's *Christmas Eve Dialogue*: Bourgeois Ideology or Feminist Theology?', *Journal of Religion* 69, 1989, 169–83, taking issue with Massey's less positive interpretation in *Feminine Soul* (n.21), ch. 6.

25. I have presented some preliminary thoughts on this issue in S. Coakley, 'Creaturehood before God, Male and Female', *Theology* 93, 1990, 343–53. Cf. also n. 15 above.

26. For an important recent discussion of the heritage of the Enlightenment for feminism, see S. Lovibond, 'Feminism and Postmodernism', *New Left Review* 178, 1989, 5–28.

III · Critical Feminist Theological Exploration

'Woman's Special Nature': A Different Horizon for Theological Anthropology

Katherine E. Zappone

Why do we want to know if 'woman' has a 'special nature'? What are the theological (and other) interests that crowd behind this question, pushing it to centre-stage of feminist discourse? Initially, the focus on woman's nature was propelled by a very practical concern. Traditional theological reflection had defined woman as different from and inferior to man. Woman's 'specialness' really meant woman's confinement to secondary status and specified social roles. Woman's dignity, equality and freedom were at stake. So feminist theologians criticized past definitions and initiated the long journey of trying to answer: is woman different from man in a different way than man had thought? Is she different yet just as worthy, equal and free?

That's where it all began, yet other interests soon surfaced as the question of woman's special nature fired the creativity of feminist theology. If we could name woman's experience of being human, then we could critique a theological tradition built on man's experience of being human. If we could identify the characteristics of woman's innate nature, then we could state clearly the kinds of contributions that she has to offer to the public domain. The direction of our planet has not fared well with men in control of the public. Perhaps women's experiences and special nature could shift the social patterns of oppression, famine and war. However, in the midst of these interests and questions theologians ran into the same sorts of dilemmas that feminists within other disciplines were attempting to resolve. What determines woman's nature? Is it biology, socio-cultural expectations, or historical experiences? Does biology affect innate characteristics, and predispose us towards certain social roles? Is woman 'closer to nature' than man?

A pivotal point in the discussion was signalled by Audre Lorde's 1980 publication of the essay 'Age, Race, Class and Sex: Women Redefining Difference'. Describing herself at the time as a 'forty-nine-year-old Black lesbian feminist socialist mother of two, including one boy, and a member of an inter-racial couple',[1] Lorde voiced a turning-point insight: women's difference from one another is *as significant* as their difference from men. Feminists must recognize and incorporate the meaning of these differences into their theories if they are interested in the dignity, equality and freedom of *all* women. The self-naming of 'woman' could not be done by a homogeneous group. Quite a task lay ahead.

I want to look at how the question of 'woman's nature' from a feminist perspective revolutionizes theological anthropology. I intend to highlight some of the significant shifts in content and methodological approaches that feminist theory brings to the theological understanding of the nature and destiny of the human person.[2] My own interests are both practical and theoretical. As a United States American making my primary home in Ireland, and as one learning and teaching in the midst of class differences, I am constantly wondering how to live with difference in ways that contribute to the overall creative/salvific process. As a theologian I am convinced that the concern for the distinctiveness and diversity of women offers one of the most imaginative tools to create theory that originates from and continues to make a difference.

Women's experience and human nature

Attention to 'women's experience' was one of the first ways that feminist theologians sought to redefine human nature. In 1960 Valerie Saiving wrote a watershed article that changed the course of theology and its anthropology. Her essay galvanized feminist inquiry for several reasons. By arguing that 'feminine' experience is essentially different from 'masculine' experience, she was able to criticize theological statements about the universal nature of sin as the 'unjustified concern of the self for its own power and prestige' and love as 'completely self-giving, taking no thought for its own interests but seeking only the good of the other'.[3] These may be definitions of sin and love from man's perspective but, Saiving argued, they did not apply to woman. In effect, she challenged the possibility of making universal claims about human nature by attending only to the experience of one half of the human race. And she was one of the first to describe the structure of 'feminine' experience in order to demonstrate its theological import.

Judith Plaskow chose Saiving's foundational insights to frame a more nuanced understanding of how women's experience undercuts universal meanings of sin and grace.[4] Contrary to Saiving, however, Plaskow argued that women do not always and everywhere possess similar essential characteristics. Saiving had proposed that 'feminine' experience was *directly* affected by biology; the female was naturally more passive and less anxious than the male, and she was more focussed on *being* than *becoming*. Plaskow said no. Anthropologists and other social scientists had demonstrated that cultural factors affect woman's sense of herself far more than physiological ones do. Consequently she identified the content of women's experience through an analysis of what the culture expects and how women live in relation to these expectations. This provided Plaskow with a base to suggest that women's sin is more aptly described as self-negation (rather than self-assertion), and self-realization (rather than selfless love) is her grace-filled process.

Judith Plaskow's enduring contribution, I think, lies in her willingness to acknowledge that 'I am . . . not arguing for the universality of my own definition of women's experience . . . My view . . . is one view of modern, white, western, middle-class women's experience.'[5] Women theologians ought to be just as careful as men theologians in their attempts to make universal claims. This leaves the door wide open to theorize not only from the perspective of women's difference from men but also with attention to women's differences from one another. Those who hold a strict 'essentialist' position cannot adequately heed both kinds of difference. Therefore I want to turn now to selected feminist theorists who describe ways to focus on both differences, and explore how this affects the shape of theological anthropology.

Does biology affect women's destiny?

As I've already indicated, the subject matter of theological anthropology has a lot to do with human destiny. How should we behave, what ought we to be doing, what virtues will we embody so that human praxis creates and heals with God? In much of past theological and ecclesial reflection, woman's 'special nature' – solidly rooted in the biological capacity for childbearing – meant that her destiny was to sanctify the domestic sphere. Still today in Ireland, Article 41 of the Constitution (written under the influence of Catholic social teaching[6]) legitimizes this concept of woman's destiny:

The State recognizes the Family as the natural primary and fundamental unit group of Society . . . The State, therefore, guarantees to protect the Family in its constitution and authority . . . In particular, the State recognizes that by her life within the home, woman gives to the State a support without which the common good cannot be achieved. The State shall, therefore, endeavour to ensure that mothers shall not be obliged by economic necessity to engage in labour to the neglect of their duties in the home.

This socio-legal reality provides a very concrete example of why feminist theory must take another look at the relation between sex (that is, biological differences between female and male) and destiny.

Janet Sayers' work, *Biological Politics*,[7] offers a constructive thesis regarding this connection and, I think, one that also maintains real differences between women. Her central thesis is this: biology – *as it interacts with socio-economic and historical factors* – directly affects women's experience and how they live roles within the social order. She argues against the feminist position of 'biological essentialism', namely, that biology endows women with an essential and particular 'feminine' character. When applied to the societal role of 'motherhood', the essentialist theory proffers that women are in fact better equipped to nurture children than men. Women's equality will be achieved, then, not through the open choice of social roles but through a radical shift in the culture's valuation of mothering. Sayers claims that this *idea* does not take adequate account of the *material* differences between women. Motherhood, without access to economic independence, is not necessarily a positive and uniform experience for all women, nor will it automatically transform a patriarchal culture.

So, does biology make any difference at all? Yes, Sayers maintains, and for this reason also criticizes the feminist theory of 'social constructionism' which puts the case that 'the influence of biology on women's status is . . . indirect, . . . it is mediated by the way their biology is interpreted and construed within a given society.'[8] Sayers argues that this theory reduces the importance of how individual women experience their biological differences from men. For example, she looks at how various women interpret the biological reality of menstruation. Does the experience of menstruation affect women's potential to work? The social constructionist thesis – put forward by middle-class women – argues that only the negative social attitudes towards menstruation, not the biological experience itself, restricts women's professional capabilities. Therefore they make the case that women pilots, doctors or lawyers are not inhibited in their competence and effectiveness because of menstruation. This theory denies, however, that some women's experience of menstruation is negative and physically debilitating (regardless of the use of medication). Sayers points out that women working in low-paid industrial jobs have not benefitted from this denial of direct biological effect. Working-class women seeking to garner possibilities of dispensation from work due to menstrual pain have been blocked by claims that the effects of menstruation are socially and psychologically constructed, not physiologically real. Similar to biological essentialism, this position does not serve the interest of *all* women.

How can this analysis benefit theological anthropology? Initially it contributes to the deconstruction of the patriarchal ideology of woman's 'special nature'. As Beverly Harrison persuasively argues, 'advanced capitalist industrial development needs the social myth of women's "special nature and place" to keep women out of productive work or, failing that, out of the labour movement . . .'⁹ Article 41 of the Irish Constitution clearly demonstrates the socio-economic implications of such a myth. My own work with women who experience poverty confirms that the concept of 'special nature' – even in the feminist version of essentialist theory – reinforces their entrapment in a cycle of extraordinary suffering. However, Sayers' analysis offers something more. By examining women's experience with attention to the vast differences in women's lives, we can still claim that biology does affect women's (and men's) destiny. It *does not*, however, affect the course of our lives by taking choices from us. Instead, it's by the way in which those biological differences interact with other cultural, social and historical realities that human choice is restricted (or enhanced).

Perhaps we can say of human nature, then, that we ought to be able to exercise choice through and with biological differences. Our femaleness or maleness directly affects the ways that we conceive and nurture one another. Our choices with reference to these activities always happen, though, within the confines of race, class, sexual orientation and culture. Our creative response to biological difference as it interacts with these other factors is what contributes to the creative/salvific process. This response may be not so much the transcendence of biology as it is the reconstruction of social relations and systems that make biology a prison for women. What this points to as well is the powerful nature of the human person. But our power to effect change for the good of the common (which necessarily includes ourselves) cannot happen without a communal orientation that respects the differences among us. Grace – like sin – may be better conceived of as a social reality. The feminist focus on different kinds of women's experiences challenges an individualist conceptualization of every theological category.

To what extent does 'difference' make a difference?

I have argued that attention to both biology and socio-cultural factors ought to be part of a feminist theological redefinition of human nature. This would mean that differences between men and women, and differences between women, shape the starting-point of our theory-building. What this requires of us, first and foremost, is the ability to move beyond the fear of 'difference' as an analytic category. Let me suggest a couple of reasons why we carry this fear. Within a patriarchal socio-cultural framework, to describe someone as different usually means that she or he is different *from the norm*. Consequently difference carries with it the implication of inferiority and inequality. And even though the patriarchs say woman is 'different but equal', this naming only masks assumed inferiority because woman's difference is being defined for her. If we move beyond this fear by women naming themselves, we meet another one. A feminist description of woman's difference from man initially offered a white, middle-class, Western perspective as if it were true for all women. To accept the 'difference among women' as part of our starting point means that we will have to be self-critical as well as critical. It will challenge the theory that many of us struggled hard to create. And it will relativize the universalizing attempts of women who hold dominance in terms of class, culture, sexual orientation and/or race.

If I accept the challenge to move beyond both kinds of fears, then a stated awareness of the diversity of women's experiences will be only the initial step to mine the extent that 'difference' as starting-point can make. Henrietta Moore, in her book *Feminism and Anthropology*, identifies the next and considerably more significant step. She posits that 'universal woman' does not exist. She outlines the sociological deconstruction of 'woman' by showing that it is an analytic category with no meaning. There is no way to describe 'woman' (or 'man') that incorporates attention to the real differences between women (or men). As an anthropologist she is acutely sensitive to how the meaning of 'woman' changes from culture to culture. Therefore 'gender', namely, the *meaning* attached to sex differences, is a more adequate analytic category than 'woman'. 'Gender' enables cultural difference to be taken into account. But feminist theory, she claims, must also recognize that there are many differences among women within the same culture. It is not sufficient to say that gender identity is shaped by culture alone. Race and class also radically affect the experience of being female within a given culture. Gender, then, can't be analysed on its own. Feminist anthropology ought to describe how race and class are experienced through gender. Being woman is inseparable from being the kind of woman one is.[10]

When we come to reflect theologically about the nature of humanity with women's experiences as one of the primary sources, it is no longer enough to focus exclusively on the difference gender makes. Our analysis should begin with and consistently incorporate the realities that are named out of the diverse backgrounds of women. Susan Thistlethwaite follows this kind of method as she examines how race and gender make an impact on theological anthropology.[11] She challenges white feminists to study womanist (black women's) theory. This provides not only a corrective to the white feminist tendency to make universal claims for all women, but also demonstrates the disparity between black women's theory and white women's theory. For example, Thistlethwaite considers the difference between white feminist and womanist theory regarding nature and creation. Whereas white feminist theory tends to emphasize the harmonious, good and creative aspects of nature, womanist reflection focuses more on the conflictual and destructive nature of nature. She points out that 'according to many womanists . . . the creation is *fallen*, sin and evil are stunningly real and there is no (easy?) access to harmony'.[12] Whereas white feminists tend to identify nature as good and culture as bad, black women's literature demonstrates how race affects women's experience of nature: it destroys as well as nurtures in the lives of those who constantly face the harsh realities of racism and poverty. Therefore black women's healing does not entail the search for experiences of unity with the natural world as much as struggling to change the social systems that keep the destructive sides of nature at their doorsteps. A key question surfaces: how does this concept of healing critique white feminist theology? At the least white theological efforts to understand the interdependence of humanity with the natural world ought not to exclude black reflection identifying nature's independence and destructive potential. On the horizon, though, may be a completely different way of naming the nature of creation. And, this might bring us closer to representing more accurately the way things 'really are', as well as provide effective strategies for healing humanity and the world.

Acknowledging and incorporating difference is far more than a theoretical adventure, though. Its value does not lie in the theoretical realm only. The praxis of living with difference, namely, stepping outside the racial, sexual, cultural and/or class separations that we inherit, provides a grace-filled path to know, respect and love the difference. My experience of crossing class and culture boundaries reveals first of all the superiority complexes that come with being American and middle-class. It shows me sides of evil and oppression that I could never see within my own secure circles. Likewise, it manifests the extraordinary virtues that are fired within the daily task to survive. Above all it teaches me how to cope creatively with the inherent conflicts of difference rather than ignore or obliterate them. In this I discover the meaning of 'solidarity' and its significance for political change that will benefit myself and women who are not like me at all. 'Solidarity' or 'sisterhood' with real power is not possible without the struggle to explore and respect differences.

The praxis of living with difference, in turn, profoundly motivates the theoretical method outlined above. But where ultimately does all of this lead? We've travelled far beyond the question of 'woman's special nature'. That's what makes it such a good one and explains why we ought to continue asking it. Implicit in all of the discussion, though, is not simply the affirmation that women's experiences supplement theological anthropology. I am also saying that this source makes it *better*. Yes, feminist theology has made this claim since its origins. But we need to refine this assertion in the light of the focus on difference. If we say that it is necessary to theorize from the perspective of difference, how can we say anything that means something to someone else? Or, how can our theory which is rooted in the particular experiences of different women, be true for all women and men? With reference to the present topic, how can we make better statements about the nature of being human if we don't take account of every woman's particular experience?

These are hard questions. They form a contemporary variation on the inherited philosophical theme of the relation between particular experience and universal truth. Sara Ruddick's discussion of her own universalizing tendency is a significant contribution to the present quandary.[13] She is aware of the philosophical and feminist mood of difference. She knows, for example, that the experience of mothering is dependent on a person's social, cultural and historical location. Still, she insists that it is possible to delineate the content of what she names 'maternal thinking'. Ruddick proposes that there are ways of knowing and a body of knowledge that surface within the practice of anyone who 'mothers'. She defines the practice of mothering as taking responsibility for meeting children's demands of preservation, nurturance and social acceptability. By drawing on her own experience of mothering, and by listening to the stories and theories of many others who have mothered, Ruddick identifies ways of thinking that are common to every 'mother'. For example, she defines one such form of maternal thinking as 'holding'.

> To hold means to minimize risk and to reconcile differences rather than to sharply accentuate them. Holding is a way of seeing with an eye toward maintaining the minimal harmony, material resources, and skills necessary for maintaining a child in safety.[14]

She also argues that maternal thinking is better than the dominant discourse of militaristic thinking. Maternal – not militaristic – thinking opens the gateway towards the politics of authentic peace.

Let us return to our question: how can we make better statements about the nature of being human if we do not take account of every woman's experience? Applying Ruddick's theoretical practice, we first look for common features in the midst of listening to difference among women. The search for commonality necessarily entails the process of criticizing and being criticized by theories that come from social and historical locations that are different from our own. It entails a socio-economic, cultural and racial analysis as well as a psychological one. Then our description of what's common and familiar – perhaps even universal – is based on the assumption of difference, not sameness.

The heart of the matter has to do with *why* we want to describe what is common. It cannot come from the wish – however unconscious – to negate difference. In referring to the mothering practice of a rural woman, Ruddick says, 'The identification in protective work that I feel and claim with that farm woman cannot depend on my being *like* her. Nor do I aspire to replace a description of her work and thinking with a generalized version of my own.'[15] Instead, Ruddick insists that we must continue to collect the different stories of mothering (or, the different stories of women's experiences), while at the same time positing what is common among them in order to correct past ways of thinking about peace (or, past ways of theologizing about human nature). The universal aspects of women's different experiences provide the base to assert that 'this is the way things really are'. The cumulative analyses – not the scattered interpretations of different experiences – have the power to challenge the dominant discourse.

How will we know that these theories about sin and grace, creation and redemption, are better? First, we will need consistently to be vigilant about the kinds of practices that they encourage. We will have to test continuously their 'truth-in-action'.[16] Will they encourage ways to behave so that no one is violated? Will they show us how to survive our differences? At the same time we will need to incorporate humility and provisionality in our theory-making. Ruddick refers to the notion of looking for a 'cumulative universality' rather than an absolute universality.[17] We can never say that our theology about human nature is absolutely true. This does not allow for the possibility of revising our practices because of different experiences that have not yet been voiced. Anne Carr is correct when she says that our idea of human nature ought to keep changing.[18] Ruddick with disarming honesty offers a metaphor that is helpful in this regard. Though she theorizes about what is common amidst the differences, she admits that 'I am one reader, observer and mother', and 'I make it up'.[19] After all our research, listening and practice, we, too, 'make it up'.

The question of 'woman's special nature' is significant not simply because it provokes gender, race and class analysis; its importance lies also in creating a new theological horizon with colours and textures never highlighted before.

Notes

1. From Audre Lorde, *Sister Outsider: Essays and Speeches*, Trumansburg, NY 1984, 114.
2. See also Anne Carr's fine examination of feminism and theological anthropology in *Transforming Grace: Christian Tradition and Women's Experience*, San Francisco 1988, 117–33.
3. Valerie Saiving, 'The Human Situation: A Feminine View', in *Womanspirit Rising*, ed. Carol Christ and Judith Plaskow, San Francisco 1979, 26.
4. Judith Plaskow, *Sex, Sin and Grace: Women's Experience and the Theologies of Reinhold Niebuhr and Paul Tillich*, Washington DC 1980.
5. Ibid., 6.
6. See Liam Dowd's analysis of how Catholic teaching radically affected this and several other aspects of the composition of the 1937 Constitution in his essay, 'Church, State and Women: The Aftermath of Partition', in *Gender in Irish Society*, ed. Chris Curtin, Pauline Jackson, Barbara O'Connor, Galway 1987, 3–36.
7. Janet Sayers, *Biological Politics: Feminist and Anti-Feminist Perspectives*, London 1982.
8. Ibid., 3.
9. Beverly Harrison, in *Making the Connections*, ed. Carol Robb, Boston 1985, 52. See also Elisabeth Schüssler Fiorenza's analysis of how Aristotle provides a philosophical justification for two kinds of human nature because the socio-political structures of Athenian democracy require it, 'Breaking the Silence: Becoming Visible', *Concilium* 182, 1985, 5–7.
10. Henrietta Moore, *Feminism and Anthropology*, Cambridge 1988, 1–11, 186–98. Moore, however, does not pay sufficient attention to how biology directly affects women's experiences. She accepts the general trend within anthropology that 'what cultures make of sex differences is almost infinitely variable, so . . . biology cannot play a determining role' (p. 7). While gender may be constructed differently within different cultures, this does not take away the possibility that each woman interprets for herself – within the context of her socio-economic status – the meaning of her biology. Part of the meaning of sex differences (gender) comes from the influence of biology. For example, as Sayers points out, the experience of pregnancy may be experienced by some women as the growth of a parasite within them, while by other women it may be experienced as the growth of an extension of themselves. Differences in interpretation – due to the personal makeup of the woman – will affect the kind of 'motherly' activity and characteristics that the woman manifests (see Sayers, pp. 147–72). Anthropological – and theological – observation should continue to investigate how biological differences affect human experience.
11. Susan Thistlethwaite, *Sex, Race and God: Christian Feminism in Blake and White*, New York 1989.
12. Ibid., 61.

13. Sara Ruddick, *Maternal Thinking: Toward a Politics of Peace*, Boston 1989, especially 51–7, 127–40.

14. Ibid., 78–9.

15. Ibid., 52.

16. Thistlethwaite, *Sex, Race and God* (n.11), 24–6.

17. Ruddick, *Maternal Thinking* (n.13), 259–60.

18. Carr, *Transforming Grace* (n.2), 131–33.

19. Ruddick, *Maternal Thinking* (n.13), 61.

Woman: Time and Eternity
The Eternal Woman and the Feminine
Face of God

Maria Clara Luchetti Bingemer

Theological reflection from the woman's viewpoint has recently been attempting to explore the difficult but nonetheless challenging subject of the concept and image of God. The starting point of this reflection has been the fact that Christianity, in the different cultures in which it has sunk roots, has always given preference to masculine names and perspectives in identifying the God of which it speaks and to whom it refers. Nonetheless the question of the feminine element in God has arisen with increasing frequency. The reasons why the issue keeps coming up are not simply connected with the implications it raises for anthropology, which, without the feminine dimension, would be crippled, lacking one of its essential parameters for understanding the human being as the image of God. They have to do as well with theology and discussion on the identity and face of the God of the Christian faith. In terms of the content of his own self-communication, and the features of his revelation, this God cannot be identified primarily with only one of the sexes without a denial of his totality, infinity and transcendence.

In the Western church, especially in the Catholic church, there has been a tendency to look for answers to some of these questions about the feminine element in God in the mystery of Mary. In this article I shall try to show that the heavy Mariological emphasis in the Western church really derives largely from a pneumatological gap. Secondly, I shall try to find some approaches to the mystery of Mary, as a prototype not only of humanity, but particularly of the female part of humanity. I shall also try to show how this Mariological perspective, which we are trying to build on new anthropological foundations, can give women new opportunities to rediscover their identity. It can also give rise to more coherent ways of redefining the feminine dimension of God in terms of the divine trinitarian community itself, which is formed by the three-person entity invoked by the Christian people as Father, Son and Holy Spirit.

The 'absence' of the Holy Spirit in the life of the Western church

Any consideration of the 'disappearance' of the feminine element in the Christian theological conception of God ought to start with an important distinction, the evolution and the journey of trinitarian theology and reflection on the God of the Christian faith in the West and in the East.

From the very beginnings of the life of the church (the second and third centuries of the Christian era), the Eastern church maintained a harmonious balance between christology and pneumatology, with all the consequences flowing from this for ecclesiology (less rigidity and more flexibility), for spirituality (which permeated all areas of church life, even church organization, as well as liturgy, sacred art and so on), and for theological reflection itself (which recognized reason as *one* of its dimensions, but not the primary one). This made possible a theology deeply and indissolubly interwoven with spirituality and contemplation, in which symbols and poetry are guaranteed a central place.

In the West, the direct consequences, in the past and still today, of the 'loss' of such a strongly marked presence of the Holy Spirit include a christology largely detached from pneumatology, with an emphasis on a dialectical tension between the dogmatic and the historical-horizontal bordering on a christomonism, and an ecclesiology in which canonical interpretations of the 'institution' predominate in the organizational definition, and the different segments of the people of God have great difficulty in integrating this with the mystery aspect of the church in their understanding and behaviour.[1] In this context the strong point of theological reflection is its detached rationality, detached in its content, conceptual method and literary form from spirituality, symbol and poetry; the mystagogical element which ought to be present in all reflection and communication about the mystery of God is hard to detect, if not absent.[2]

The significance of this 'absence' for our present subject is that it has led in the West to a search for a 'substitute' for the presence of the Spirit and all that this implies and brings with it.[3] It is impossible to build ecclesial life without the Spirit. The work of the Spirit is to generate life, life in which gratuitousness, sensitivity, receptivity – in short, all that enchants and seduces human beings – is present. An ecclesial community whose strengths are almost exlusively rational, logical and institutional will never succeed in moving hearts and touching the deepest core of desires, in motivating people and their feelings, making them feel loved, protected, welcomed, in short, consoled.

The fact that, in our culture, all these attributes have been traditionally and culturally associated with women and femininity is another element in the picture I am trying to describe here. In addition, it goes a long way towards explaining the current difficulties in the West in including the feminine dimension in Christian theological reflection on God.

The space left empty by the absence of pneumatology was gradually occupied – in many places and for many people and communities, but above all in the popular religious imagination, and most strongly in Catholic circles – by the figure of Mary of Nazareth, our Lady, mother of Jesus and mother of God.[4] In Mary the Catholic people sought and slowly discovered what was their most hidden object of desire, the feminine and maternal face of God. It was this which finally embodied and made visible the feminine dimension – the mercy, tenderness and compassion – of the God of the Bible.[5]

Mary of Nazareth: goddess or creation of God?

The classical treatises on Mariology show very clearly this 'theological transposition' to Mary of the feminine and maternal divine dimension whose absence was felt so painfully by a large part of the people of God. The anthropologies underlying these Mariologies show the limitations from which church life in the West suffered from a very early date. They are markedly androcentric anthropologies, conceived on the basis of the human male, whom they make the model of humanity and also, therefore, the model for the image of God.[6] They are, in large part, dualist in their approach, dissociating body from spirit and giving a higher status to the latter than to the former. They separate the historical and temporal from the eternal and eschatological, setting up revelation and the history of salvation as a dimension above and beyond real, chronological, factual history, leaving no possibility of dialogue between the one and the other. They are one-dimensional, operating with definitions of the human (and therefore of the divine too) which are predetermined, closed, excluding pluridimensional and dynamic richness as a negation of what God revealed and willed.[7]

Mary of Nazareth and thinking about her, especially within Catholic theology, was deeply coloured by this anthropological and theological background, with ambiguous consequences. On the one hand, in academic and scientific theology, there developed a Mariology which in a way isolated and separated the human and the transcendent aspects of Mary, placing her more on the 'other' side of heaven, alongside the throne of the Godhead and sharing in its majesty and inaccessibility. On the other hand, among the simpler Catholic faithful, there grew up a devotion to Mary of Nazareth – our Lady of the many names, the Immaculate Conception, our Lady of Copacabana, of Luján, of Lourdes, of Fatima, Aparecida, etc. – which gradually assumed truly enormous proportions and almost replaced – at least in terms of proximity, confidence and intimacy – the relationship with Jesus Christ and God the Father himself.[8]

We must not make superficial or hasty judgments about this devotion. The simpler Catholic faithful, especially because they are poor, deprived and suffer in various aspects of their lives, seek in Mary a 'strength', a 'support', which enables them to hope, beyond any material and obvious possibility of hope, that the last word on life may not be reduced to the level of the visible and tangible of everyday history, but may find its reference in something or someone – a transcendence which reveals itself in time but is not exhausted by it – which helps them to interpret life, helps them to feel accompanied and not abandoned, however bad the circumstances and the tragedies which befall.

For these people, Mary represents and symbolizes this hope: she is mother, protector, the one who does not abandon her children and who may readily be invoked and whose presence is felt and touched in the heart's consolation, in the security brought by the recitation of litanies, by the saying of the rosary and all the invocations which popular creativity has invented. Such perfect motherhood – in the sense given to this term by culture and in the sense in which the human unconscious gives it of the archetype of the source of life always longed for by the human race – is understandably felt as more than human, as almost divine and, although this is not always said and verbalized, as *really* divine.

But does this mean losing the possibility of advancing into, exploring further, the human, creaturely, 'carnal' dimension of Mary, the one which really corresponds to the datum of revelation and the official teaching of the church? Does it mean that we close off for ever the other, enormously rich possibilities of imagining the feminine component of God, not in terms of Mary, but in terms of the three divine persons who constitute the identity of the God of the Christian faith, Father, Son and Holy Spirit? And not only that: does the exaggerated development of the Marian cult and devotion help the whole process of women's liberation which is gathering strength just as much within the church as in society in general? Can this Mary – understood more as a divine or semi-divine being than as a creature of God – provide a fruitful line of reflection on God from a woman's viewpoint which meets the aspirations of this age and its people? Finally, does this process of the 'divinization' of Mary enable this reflection on the feminine in God to be carried on as part of the ecumenical dialogue, which has become an important priority for all the Christian churches, especially in recent decades?[9]

In this article I have chosen a line of thought which may seem at first sight reductionist: to think about Mary's identity in terms of two Marian dogmas of the Catholic Church, one of them quite controversial, the Immaculate Conception, and the divine motherhood. In doing so I deliberately accept the risks involved in the hope that my choice will help to throw more light on the problems outlined above.

Mary Immaculate and the mystery of creation[10]

The Catholic dogma of the Immaculate Conception, so polemical and controversial, can, despite all the ecumenical difficulties caused by its theological, moral and ecclesial implications, tell us something about the subject we are considering, the idea of the feminine in God.

First, in anthropological terms, the dogmatic formula implies an integrated and unified concept of the human person.[11] It is not just Mary's soul which is preserved from sin and opposition to God's plan. It is her whole person, penetrated and energized by the divine life, her bodiliness as the dwelling of the holy God, the place in which the Spirit of God rests and pitches her tent. For all that she is the unblemished fruit of God's creation, Mary is, in this view, more than ever a daughter of earth. Though she is the dwelling of the fullness of the splendour of the Spirit of God, she remains rooted in history and in the specificity of the human condition, which she has never ceased to share.[12]

The female body, which was for so many centuries regarded by large sections of the church – on the basis of a dubious interpretation of the Genesis story – as the cause of original sin, something which left the whole female sex with a heavy burden of guilt, is rehabilitated by the Catholic Church when it declares blessed this female body animated by the divine Spirit.[13] In this flesh and in the person of this woman, God the creator triumphantly achieved the climax of his wonders, and the human race was able to see its vocation and destiny as creation brought to a successful conclusion.

As a 'daughter of Zion', Mary represents the people of Israel, of which she is a legitimate child. In her the journey of the covenant of this people with its God reaches its climax. As a faithful Israelite, who waits for the consolation of the chosen people and sings of the wonders the Lord performs, recognizing his life-producing presence in her and around her, Mary is the prototype of the people of God of yesterday and today, showing that people its vocation, as chosen 'before the world was made to be holy and faultless' (Eph. 1.4).

Catholic theology's view of Mary of Nazareth is therefore that she is a prototype of the creature and not a goddess. In her creaturely condition, she can proclaim to the sons and daughters of God the greatness of their vocation and the possibility of its full realization. In her, God the creator manifests all his wonders and the whole potential of his creative and constantly life-producing dream. Remaining a creature, in close alliance with her brothers and sisters of flesh and election, she points to the mystery of creation in which men and women understand themselves to be in alliance with the cosmos and open themselves to the boundlessness of the divine.

The miracle and mystery of her creation point, not to her, but to the One who created her and reveals himself, not just as loving Father, creator of heaven and earth and all that exists, but also as the Mother who gives birth and nurtures the fruit of her womb. While described in the Bible as a powerful Lord, a mighty warrior, the Father who begets, the God of Israel, Mary's God is at the same time a God of mercy and tenderness, whose compassion remains from generation to generation, and whose compassionate entrails are described in the same words used to describe the female womb, which moves, writhes and groans in pains of anguish for the sons and daughters it has borne.[14]

Mary, the prototype of the creature in which God finds complete freedom to reveal himself in the world, reveals the face of that Maternal Father whom Jesus of Nazareth was to teach us to call affectionately *Abba*. This motherly Father, the mystery of life, begetting and giving birth, takes part and involves himself passionately in the sufferings of his people, lives among the lowly and powerless and sends his Son to take flesh in the womb of the woman Mary.[15]

The Theotokos and the mystery of the incarnation[16]

The first great truth of faith which the church proclaims about Mary is that she is the mother of God. In the Gospels, Mary is fundamentally the mother of Jesus, and the church, at the Council of Ephesus in 431, proclaimed her solemnly *Theotokos*, 'mother of God'.

To recognize Mary as the mother of God means to profess that her son, the carpenter from Nazareth, the man who was crucified, is the Son of God and God himself. Now, every woman who is a mother is the mother, not just of the body, but of the whole person of the child she bears and carries for nine months in her womb, nourishing it afterwards with the milk produced and created from within her own body. Since it is impossible to separate humanity and divinity in Jesus Christ, it is also impossible to separate in Mary the simple woman from Nazareth and her whom the church venerates and worships as the mother of God.

Through the mystery of the incarnation of God, the central mystery of the Christian faith, of which the mystery of the *Theotokos* is an integral part, we can say that the greatness and the infinity of the Holy Spirit are to be found only in the fragility, poverty and limitations of human flesh. Mary's flesh, which wove and formed in her womb, cell by cell, what was to be the human flesh of the Word of God, is an integral part of the mystery of the incarnation.

The fact that God became flesh in a male has been the basis of much talk and many claims designed to reinforce the supremacy of men over women in the church. The deepest content of this central mystery of the Christian faith, however, is not that God became man, but that he became flesh, human flesh.[17] While, at the beginning of the process of the human generation of the Word of God, the divine Spirit was the sole agent moulding and making pregnant the untouched flesh of Mary, the slow, progressive and patient weaving of the bodiliness of the Word once formed took place in Mary's womb. Her flesh gradually formed and gave flesh to the Word of God, day by day, moment by moment, in the mysterious body-to-body dialogue which touches the furthest and deepest roots of life.

It is this bodiliness of the man Jesus, formed and woven in the entrails of the woman Mary by the power of the Holy Spirit, which went around the world doing miracles, curing the sick, raising the dead, multiplying loaves, being hated, persecuted, tortured and crucified. He also proclaimed, finally and irreversibly, the alliance between flesh and spirit made for ever possible by the mercy of God.

At the centre of this supreme mystery which transforms the meaning of history and becomes the primary criterion for judging past, present and future is human flesh. It is man's flesh and woman's flesh, the flesh of Jesus of Nazareth, Word of God incarnate by the power of the Spirit, true God and true man, the flesh of the woman Mary, bodiliness open to the invasion of the Spirit and human possibility of the body of God incarnate in history. The Word of God became flesh in human flesh, male and female flesh, flesh marked historically by space and time, by life and death, by joy and pain, by growth and destruction, in short by all the conflicts inherent in human existence and history.[18]

Woman, therefore, is at the very centre of the Christian mystery in the person of Mary of Nazareth. This is not the icon Mary, whom people have so often tried to separate from her flesh and make a purely spiritualized projection, but Mary who unveils in her person the whole mystery of womanhood, the mystery of openness, of being source and protector of life. She is a woman linked, like every woman, and much more than any other, to the procreation and mystery of life.

Mother of Jesus and mother of God, Mary is at the same time the fully human revelation of an unknown and unexplored side of the very mystery of God, incarnate in her womb. This God is, essentially, life and life in abundance, who compares himself, in the biblical revelation, to the woman who gives birth and suckles the child of her womb (cf. Isa. 66.13; 42.14; 49.15), and shows his face in Mary of Nazareth. It is from this woman's flesh that he takes his flesh in Jesus the Son.

Conclusion: neither goddess nor eternal woman

The 'substitution' performed by the practice of the Western church, in giving heavy emphasis to the person of Mary as a result of the felt absence of the Holy Spirit and therefore of a coherent pneumatology, is today at a crossroads. On the one hand, the return of pneumatology to the forefront of discussion in church and theology brings new opportunities, not only for thinking about Mary in her proper context as a creature of God totally sanctified and moulded by the Spirit, but also for thinking about the feminine element in God. This means starting, not from Mary, but from the proper place and appropriate perspective, the trinitarian divine community, in which God reveals himself as at once one and plural, as integrating all the dichotomies and inadequacies of the human state, including those which prevent a satisfactory expression of the mystery of masculinity and femininity, the mystery of difference and reciprocity.

On the other hand, this relocation of Mary in her proper place within the totality of revelation, from which she can enlighten those who believe in her and invoke her, cannot and must not bring back to the life of the church the myth of the 'eternal' feminine, which for so long imposed on women a single prototype and a single way of living their identities. As the process of personal and collective emancipation of the female gender has gone on, women have ceased to identify with the Marian model they were presented with. They no longer recognized themselves in the Mary they were offered: silent, discreet and subordinate, always saying yes, the prototype of the eternal feminine.[19]

The 'eternal' feminine is not to be found because it doesn't exist. What exists is the provisional, the diverse, the multiple, the contingent inherent in life in historical time, which appears in different moulds according to the different cultural contexts and historical periods in which they occur. In this temporal state, a woman can find inspiration in Mary, not as an ecstatic and imprisoning prototype, but as someone who lived in a temporal and human way, which constitutes the only approach to the eternity and transcendence of the true God. That God is a loving and compassionate Father and Mother, Son and Word becoming flesh in history in male and female flesh, Spirit who produces, generates and welcomes life, blows fiercely at the same time as teaching us to speak, feeding and protecting the fragile flame of life created by God.

Translated by Francis McDonagh

Notes

1. Cf J. Comblin, *The Holy Spirit and Liberation*, Maryknoll, New York and London 1989, 13–15.

2. Comblin, *The Holy Spirit*, 16. On this point see also Hans Urs von Balthasar, 'Teologia y Santidad', in *Verbum Caro*, Madrid 1971; Jon Sobrino, *Spirituality of Liberation*, Maryknoll, New York 1988, 47. See also the recent writings of D. A. Lane, *The Experience of God. An Invitation to do Theology*, New Jersey 1981, 22–3; K. Leech, *Experiencing God. Theology as Spirituality*, San Francisco 1985, 25–6. See also my article, 'Teologia e espiritualidade. Observações metodológicas sobre a abordagem teológica da obra de Inàcio de Loyola', *Perspectiva Teológica* 22, 1990, 205–20, and my book, *Em tudo amar e servir. Mística trinitária e práxis cristã em Inácio de Loyola*, São Paulo 1990.

3. I am using 'absence' here to mean lack of tangible and emphatic expression in the daily life of the church. In other words, the 'absence' is an omission on the church's part to remember the person of the Spirit, not a decision on the part of the Spirit.

4. In making this statement I realize that I am adopting yet another Catholic standpoint. I am doing this consciously and deliberately. In the course of the text I believe that I eventually converge with the ecumenical perspective, which is the one I wish to adopt here. On the importance of Mary in the Eastern Orthodox and Western Catholic traditions, see A. E. Carr, 'The Salvation of Women: Christ, Mary and the Church', in *Transforming Grace: Christian Tradition and Women's Experience*, San Francisco 1988. See also L. Boff, *The Maternal Face of God*, San Francisco and London, 1987, 11–18 and 61–103.

5. On this see Carr, 'The Salvation of Women' (n.4), 190.

6. On this see K. E. Borresen, 'L'anthropologie théologique d'Augustin et de Thomas d'Aquin', *Recherches de Science Religieuse* 69/3, 1981.

7. On this anthropological typology, cf I. Gebara and M. C. Bingemer, *Mary, Mother of God and Mother of the Poor*, Maryknoll, New York and London 1989, 1–19.

8. I stress this popular perspective because of the place from which I am writing, Latin America and, specifically, Brazil, where this devotion to Mary on the part of the

poor is impressive in its scale and importance. On this cf. the following sections in Gebara and Bingemer, *Mary*, 'The Dogmatics of the Poor' (n.7), 121–7, and 'Some Traditions of Devotion to Mary in Latin America', 147–83. Cf also A. G. Dorado, *De Maria conquistadora a Maria liberadora. Mariologia popular latinoamericana*, Santander 1988.

9. Take, for example, from a Catholic viewpoint, the immense concern with ecumenism which marked the whole of the Second Vatican Council and the period since the Council.

10. We begin our consideration proper of Mary with the dogma of the Immaculate Conception in order to stress the mystery of the creation or, more precisely, of God the creator, from which we can isolate some important features, relevant to theological reflection from a women's perspective.

11. The formula is in the Bull *Ineffabilis Deus*, promulgated on 8 December 1854 by Pope Pius IX, which says: 'We declare, pronounce and define that the doctrine which holds that the most blessed Virgin Mary from the first moment of her conception was, by the singular grace and privilege of almighty God, in view of the merits of Christ Jesus, the Saviour of the human race, was preserved immune from all stain of original sin, is revealed by God and is therefore firmly and constantly to be believed by all the faithful' (Neuner and Roos, *The Teaching of the Catholic Church*, ed. Karl Rahner, New York 1967, 325).

12. Cf. Gebara and Bingemer, *Mary* (n.7), 113, n.23. See also Carr, *Transforming Grace* (n.4), 192ff: 'Women are reclaiming Mary, in her human role, as a female symbol of serious religious power. The dogmas of the immaculate conception and the assumption are newly seen as specifically female symbols of the created freedom and the final transformation of the world for which women hope' (192).

13. Recently, in 1989, Pope John Paul II's encyclical *Mulieris Dignitatem* described the question of original sin very clearly, as not deriving primarily from woman, but, as in fact it is, the sin of the whole human race. Cf. on the encyclical M. C. Bingemer (ed.), *O mistério de Deus na mulher*, Rio de Janeiro 1990, 99–131, with commentaries by various women theologians.

14. The Hebrew word *rehem – rahamin*, the literal meaning of which is the female womb, is used in various Old Testament passages to describe the feelings and even the identity of the God of Israel. On this cf. my article, 'A Trindade a partir da perspectiva da mulher (Algumas pistas de reflexão)', *Revista Eclesiástica Brasileira* 46, 1986, 73–99.

15. The term Motherly Father, referring to the first person of the Trinity, is used by a number of reputable present-day theologians. Cf. J. Moltmann, *Concilium* 143, 1981, 51–6; L. Boff, *Trinity and Society*, New York and London 1988, 170–1.

16. The mystery of the *Theotókos* proclaims that Mary is that woman of whose flesh the flesh of God himself, made human in Jesus of Nazareth, was formed and born. Because of this, because I think it illuminating for an understanding of the mystery of the incarnation from a women's viewpoint, I have chosen to discuss it in this article.

17. It is significant that the Greek text of the Prologue to the Fourth Gospel, in referring to the incarnation of the Word, does not use the word corresponding to the human male (*aner*), but the word *sarx*, which means human flesh as a whole.

18. Gebara and Bingemer, *Mary* (n.7), 4–5.

19. On this see my article, 'Maria, a que soube dizer NÃO', *Grande Sinal* 40, no.4, 1986, 245–6.

The Maleness of Christ

Elizabeth A. Johnson

The story of Jesus of Nazareth, crucified and risen, confessed as the Christ, is at the centre of Christian faith in God. In the gracious power of Sophia-Spirit unleashed through his history and destiny, the community of disciples continuously retells and enacts that story as the story of God with us to heal, redeem and liberate all people and the cosmos itself. Good news indeed. But that good news is stifled when Jesus' maleness, which belongs to his historical identity, is interpreted as being essential to his redeeming christic function and identity. Then the Christ functions as a religious tool for marginalizing and excluding women. Let us be very clear: the fact that Jesus of Nazareth was a male human being is not in question. His sex was a constitutive element of his historical person along with other particularities such as his Jewish racial identity, his location in the world of first-century Galilee, and so on, and as such is to be respected. The difficulty arises, rather, from the way Jesus' maleness is construed in official androcentric theology and ecclesial praxis.

The effective history of Jesus' maleness

Feminist theological analysis lays bare at least three ways in which such distorted interpretation occurs.

1. Since the man Jesus is confessed to be the revelation of God, the Christ symbol points to maleness as an essential characteristic of divine being itself. This is exacerbated by exclusive use of father and son metaphors to interpret Jesus' relationship to God, and by use of the *logos*, connected in Greek philosophy with the male principle, to articulate his personal reality as God with us. 'Who has seen me has seen the Father' (John 14.9). This is taken literally to mean that the man Jesus is the incarnation of the male Logos and revealer of a male Father-God, despite the evidence in scripture and tradition that the mystery of God trans-

cends all naming and creates female reality in the divine image and likeness.

2. The belief that the Word became flesh and dwelt among us as a male indicates that thanks to their natural bodily resemblance, men enjoy a closer identification with Christ than do women. Men are not only theomorphic but, by virtue of their sex, also christomorphic in a way that goes beyond what is possible for women. Thus men alone among human beings are able to represent Christ fully. While women may be recipients of divine grace, they are unsuited to carry out christic actions publicly because of their sexual difference from his maleness. For this mentality, the idea that the Word might have become female flesh is not even seriously imaginable, so incapable of christic identity are women thought to be; and this, despite the doctrine of creation and the church's praxis and theology of baptism.

3. Given the dualism which essentially divorces male from female humanity, the maleness of Christ puts the salvation of women in jeopardy. The Christian story of salvation involves not only God's compassionate will to save but also the method by which that will is effective, namely, by plunging into sinful human history and transforming it from within. The early Christian aphorism, 'What is not assumed is not healed', sums up the insight that God's saving solidarity with humanity is what is crucial for the birth of the new creation. As the Nicene Creed confesses, '*et homo factus est*' ('and was made man'). But if in fact what is meant is *et vir factus est*; if maleness is essential for the christic role, then women are cut out of the loop of salvation, for female sexuality was not assumed by the Word made flesh. Thus, to Rosemary Radford Ruether's searching question, 'Can a male saviour save women?' interpretation of the maleness of Christ as essential can only answer 'No', despite Christian belief in the universality of God's saving intent.[1]

The effective history of the Christ symbol presents striking evidence of how an unbalanced focus on maleness distorts theology of God, Christian anthropology and the good news of salvation. To reconstruct christology it is imperative to rethink both the foundational anthropology which has led to such a fixation on maleness, and the theological meaning of the Christ symbol.

Anthropology: from a dominance of maleness to a celebration of difference

The social location of this problematic usage is an ecclesial community where official voice, vote and visibility belong by law only to men. Rising into intellectual expressions which of necessity support the *status quo*, this patriarchy is the bedrock for the androcentric construction of gender differences shaping the misuse of the maleness of Christ. Envisioning a different kind of community laced by relationships of mutuality and reciprocity allows feminist thought to design anthropology in an egalitarian gestalt, to practical and critical effect. Then the maleness of Christ is open to interpretation at once less important and more liberating.

In the beginning of this effort it was clear what model of anthropology feminist thought did not want, namely, the prevailing dualistic model which casts women and men as polar opposites, each bearing unique characteristics from which the other sex is exluded. Here male and female are related by the notion of complementarity, which rigidly predetermines the qualities each should cultivate and the roles each can play. Apart from naiveté about its own social conditioning, its reliance on stereotypes, and the denial of the wholeness of human experience which it mandates, this position functions as a smokescreen for the subordination of women since by its definition women are always relegated to the private, passive realm.[2]

In contrast to this dual anthropology, feminist thinkers at first developed a single-nature anthropology, which views sexual difference as biologically important for reproduction but not determinative of persons as such. Since the meaning of male and female is still historically emerging, each is free to develop the best of masculine or feminine characteristics in the search for wholeness, and may assume public and private roles according to their giftedness. Here the stress is on basic similarity rather than difference, to the point where differences become relatively inconsequential. Apart from its neglect of the importance of sexual embodiment, which affects far more than reproduction in the life of every person, this view also comes under criticism for tending to hold out a single human ideal, possibly androgynous, which can be destructive of genuine human variety.

On the one hand, feminist thought resists an unrelieved binary way of thinking, a sexual polarity view of human nature which inevitably leads to a dominant/subordinate pattern. On the other hand, reduction to an equality of sameness by ignoring sexual difference is also unacceptable. Two separate types of human nature, or unisex?

A way beyond the impasse is emerging beyond those options: one human nature celebrated in an interdependence of multiple differences.[3] Not a binary view of two male and female natures, predetermined for ever, nor abbreviation to a single ideal, but a diversity of ways of being human: a multi-polar set of combinations of essential human elements, of which sexuality is but one. Human existence has a multi-dimensional character.

If maleness and femaleness can be envisioned in a more wholistic context, their relationship to each other can be more rightly conceived.

All persons are constituted by a number of anthropological constants, essential elements which are intrinsic for their identity. These include relation to one's body, and hence one's sexuality, as the medium of human consciousness; relation through the body to the whole ecological network of the earth; relation to significant other persons as the matrix in which individuality arises; relation to social, political, and economic structures; conditioning by historical time and place; the play of theory in the praxis of one's culture as opposed to instinct alone; and orientation to hope and the pull of the future.[4] These constants mutually condition one another, and in their endless combinations are constitutive of the humanity of every person. Significantly change any one of them, and a different person results.

It is short-sighted to single out sexuality as always and everywhere more fundamental to concrete historical existence than any of the other constants. Take, for example, documented cases of cruelty to black slave women in the ante-bellum American south. On what basis would one tell such an abused woman that sex is more fundamental than race and the economic system of slavery in the design of her identity? Present-day African American womanist thinkers are highly critical of white feminism for overemphasizing sex discrimination to the exclusion of racial and class prejudice, from which black women also suffer. These biases are so intrinsically tied together in their experience that women of colour cannot distinguish the suffering that comes from one rather than another.[5] Another example: in older years, when sexual attraction diminishes, the biological differences between women and men recede in importance compared to the question of the resources available for living out life's last years in dignity or destitution.

Focusing on sexuality to the exclusion of other equally constitutive elements is the equivalent of using a microscope on this one key factor of human life when what is needed is a telescope to take in the galaxies of rich human difference. Sexuality must be integrated into a holistic vision of human persons instead of being made the touchstone of personal identity and thus distorted. The anthropological model of one human nature instantiated in a multiplicity of differences moves beyond the contrasting models of either sex dualism or the sameness of abstract individuals towards the celebration of diversity as entirely normal. The goal is to reorder the two-term and one-term systems into a multiple-term schema, one which allows connection in difference rather than constantly guaranteeing identity through opposition or uniformity. Respect can thus be extended to all persons in their endless combinations of anthropological constants, boundlessly concrete. And difference itself, rather than being a regrettable obstacle to community, can function as a creative community-shaping force. As the poet Audre Lorde appreciates, 'Difference is raw and powerful connection . . .'[6]

A multi-polar anthropology allows christology to integrate the maleness of Christ using interdependence of difference as a primary category, rather than emphasizing sexuality in an ideological, distorted way.

Christ: from the static image of the perfect man to the eschatological, living community

Feminist hermeneutics has blazed a trail showing how the gospel story of Jesus resists being used to justify patriarchal dominance in any form.[7] His preaching and life-style lived and breathed the opposite, creating a challenge which brought down on his head the wrath of religious and civil authority. They crucified him. In the light of this history Jesus' maleness can be seen to have a definite social significance. If a woman had preached compassionate love and enacted a style of authority that serves, she would have been greeted with a colossal shrug. Is this not what women are supposed to do by nature? But from a social position of male privilege Jesus preached and acted this way, and herein lies the summons. The cross, too, is a sturdy symbol of the 'kenosis of patriarchy', the self-emptying of male dominating power in favour of the new humanity of compassionate service and mutual empowerment.[8] The Gospel story of Jesus makes it clear that the heart of the problem is not that Jesus was male, but that more males have not been like Jesus.

What then of Christ? Clues for feminist interpretation can be found in the resurrection, wisdom christology, and the biblical symbol of the body of Christ.

The resurrection is a mystery of faith enveloped in the mystery of God. It negates a simple literalism that imagines Jesus still existing as in the days of his earthly life, only now invisible. Jesus has truly died, with all that this implies of change: he is gone from the midst of history according to the flesh. Faith in the resurrection affirms that God has the last word for this executed victim of state injustice and that word, blessedly, is life. Jesus with all his historicity is raised into glory by the power of the Spirit. What this ringing affirmation precisely means is inconceivable. His life is now hidden in the holy mystery of God, while his presence is known only through the Spirit wherever two or three gather, bread is broken, the hungry fed. But this indicates a transformation of his humanity so profound that it escapes our imagination. The humility of the apophatic approach acknowledges that language about the maleness of Christ at this point proceeds under the negating sign of analogy, more dissimilar than similar to any maleness known in history.

New Testament wisdom christology construes Christ Jesus in terms of the powerful female figure of Sophia who is creator, redeemer and divine renewer of the people of Israel, and indeed of the whole earth (Wisdom 7.10). Speaking her words, doing her deeds, and encountering her rejection, Jesus is depicted as the child of Sophia, her prophet, and ultimately even her incarnation (Luke 11.49 and Matt. 23.34; John 1). It is this identification which links the crucified prophet to the very creation of the world, and sets the church's feet on the road to Nicaea. The christology of Jesus Sophia shatters the male dominance carried in exclusive language about Jesus as the eternal male Logos or Son of the Father, enabling articulation of even a high incarnational christology in strong and gracious female metaphors.[9]

From the beginning, Christians are marked by the confession that Jesus Sophia is the Christ, the anointed, the blessed one. But this confession also witnesses to the truth that the beloved community shares in this christhood, participates in the living and dying and rising of Christ to such an extent that it too has a christomorphic character. Challenging a naive physicalism which collapses the totality of the Christ into the human man Jesus, metaphors such as the Body of Christ (I Cor. 12.12–27) and the branches abiding in the vine (John 15.1–11) expand the reality of Christ to include all of redeemed humanity, sisters and brothers, still on the way. Amid the suffering and conflicts of history, members of the community of disciples are *en christo* and their own lives assume a christic pattern. Biblical cosmic christology expands the notion of Christ still further (Col. 1.15–20), seeing that the universe itself is destined to be christomorphic in a reconciled new heaven and new earth.[10]

Women as 'imago Christi'

The fundamental egalitarianism of the baptism and martyrdom traditions bears out women's character as *imago Christi* in ways that are newly appreciated. One in Christ Jesus, baptized women precisely in their female bodily existence and not apart from it are clothed with Christ (Gal 3.27–28). Paul makes the meaning of this identification highly precise, using the evocative idea of image/icon. Hope makes us act with great boldness, he writes, for we unveil our faces to gaze right at Christ. Then through the power of the Spirit 'all of us are being transformed into that same image from one degree of glory to another' (II Cor. 3.18). The inclusive 'all of us' makes clear that the whole community, women as well as men, are gifted with the transformation 'into the same image', in Greek the same *eikon*, that is, the image/icon of Christ. Another example: in God's design the community is called 'to be conformed to the image' of Christ (Rom. 8.29). The Greek is instructive, for the members of the community are identified as *sym-morphos* to the *eikon*, that is, sharing the form of the likeness, or formed according to the image of Christ. No distinction on the basis of sex is made, or needed. Being christomorphic is not a sex-distinctive gift. The image of Christ does not lie in sexual similarity to the human man Jesus, but in coherence with the narrative shape of his compassionate, liberating life in the world, through the power of the Spirit. Theologically, the capacity of women and men to be *sym-morphos* to the *eikon* of Christ is identical.

A similar assessment of women in the image of Christ runs through discourse about those who suffer for the faith. In one stunning narrative Luke makes this christomorphism explicit:

> But Saul, still breathing threats and murder against the disciples of the Lord, went to the high priest and asked him for letters to the synagogues at Damascus, so that if he found any belonging to the Way, men or women, he might bring them bound to Jerusalem.

When the light from heaven flashes, when the voice asks 'Why do you persecute *me*?', when Saul wonders 'Who are you, Lord?', the momentous answer comes: 'I am Jesus, whom you are persecuting' (Acts 9.1–5). Persecuted women are here explicitly identified with Jesus, as are men, without distinction. Saul's murderous intent and tormenting actions against women disciples are actions against Christ, without qualification.

Writing on the martyrs centuries later, Vatican II continues this long-standing tradition of interpretation. Martyrdom transforms a disciple into an intense image of Christ, *imago Christi*, for the martyr 'perfects that image even to the shedding of blood'.[11] In this conciliar text no distinctions are made on the basis of the martyrs' sex, nor should there be. The four North American church women murdered in El Salvador in 1980 and the six university Jesuits with their housekeeper and her daughter killed a decade later all give a witness in the uniqueness of their own persons and circumstances that is theologically identical.

The baptismal liturgy to this very day enacts the reality that the fundamental capacity to be icons of Christ is a gift not restricted by sex; women are the Body of Christ. The martyrdom tradition recognizes that in the giving of their lives women are christomorphic in a most profound and graphic way. The practical and critical effect of this gospel truth breaks any intrinsic connection between maleness and Christ, and arrives as a challenge to patriarchal rule.

The maleness of Jesus in the whole Christ

Key elements of a feminist christology have been assembled, although not yet synthesized. In that synthesis the symbol of Christ the redeemer will take its place, but its symbolic nexus will change, expanding to include symbols drawn from female experience.[12] Without the blinders of dualistic anthropology, the Christ symbol itself will be interpreted inclusively and eschatologically. In the power of the Spirit the story of Jesus lets loose a history of discipleship equally among women and men, which goes forward in anticipatory fragments of healing and liberation. Amid a multiplicity of differences Jesus' maleness is appreciated as intrinsically important for his own personal historical identity and the historical challenge of his ministry, but not theologically determinative of his identity as the Christ nor normative for the identity of the Christian community. In the power of Sophia-Spirit women and men are christo-morphic, as are black and white, old and young, Jew and Greek, and the cosmos itself, all on the way to the new heaven and the new earth. Ideally, if the equal human dignity of women is ever recognized in ecclesial theory and praxis, this discussion about the maleness of Christ will fade away. In a more just church it would never have become such an issue.

Notes

1. R. Ruether, *Sexism and God-Talk: Toward a Feminist Theology*, Boston and London 1983, 116–38.

2. For this and the following model see A. Carr, *Transforming Grace: Women's Experience and Christian Tradition*, San Francisco 1988, 117–33; and M. A. O'Neill, 'Toward a Renewed Anthropology', *Theological Studies* 36, 1975, 725–36.

3. See M. Marx Ferree and B. Hess (eds.), *Analyzing Gender: Pespectives from the Social Sciences*, Beverly Hills, CA 1987; J. Scott, 'Deconstructing Equality-Versus-Difference', *Feminist Studies* 14, Spring 1988, 33–50. Theological use of this model is clear in R. Chopp, *The Power to Speak: Feminism, Language, God*, New York 1989.

4. E. Schillebeeckx, *Christ*, New York and London 1980, 731–43.

5. B. Hooks, *Ain't I A Woman? Black Women and Feminism*, Boston 1981; and a response by S. Thistlethwaite, *Sex, Race, and God: Christian Feminism in Black and White*, New York 1989.

6. A. Lorde, *Sister Outsider*, Freedom, CA 1984, 112.

7. See E. Schüssler Fiorenza, *In Memory of Her: A Feminist Theological Recon-*

struction of Christian Origins, New York and London 1983; R. Nakashima Brock, *Journeys by Heart: A Christology of Erotic Power*, New York 1988.

8. R. Ruether, *Sexism and God-Talk* (n.1), 137.

9. E. Johnson, 'Jesus, the Wisdom of God: A Biblical Basis for a Non-Androcentric Christology', *Ephemerides Theologicae Lovaniensis* 61, 1985, 261–94.

10. Elisabeth Schüssler Fiorenza, 'Wisdom Mythology and the Christological Hymns of the New Testament', in Robert Wilken (ed.), *Aspects of Wisdom in Judaism and Early Christianity*, Notre Dame, IN 1975, 17–41.

11. *Lumen Gentium* 42.

12. See retrieval by M. Grey, *Feminism, Redemption and the Christian Tradition*, Mystic, CN 1990.

Contributors

INA PRAETORIUS was born in Karlsruhe and studied Protestant theology and German in Tübingen, Zurich and Heidelberg. From 1983 to 1987 she was an academic assistant in the Institute for Social Ethics in the University of Zurich. At present she teaches for the theological faculty of the University of Berne and is a freelance writer and researcher. She is married to a pastor in a small country community in Switzerland, and has a daughter. Her writings include 'Geschlechtsspezifische Arbeitsteilung als theologisches Problem', *Theologia Practica* 2, 1987, 136–44; 'Feministische Ethik. Eine Einführung', in *Offene Kirche* 5, November 1988, 2–7; 'Withdrawal of Care: Feminist Ethics and Natural Science', *Concilium* 203, 1989, 5–62; 'Der kleine Unterschied zwischen Mutter und Retorte, oder Vom Frauenbild des (Natur-)Wissenschaftlers', in Jürg von Ins and Peter Grossmann (eds.), *Künstliche Leben – ärtztliche Kunst*, Zurich 1989, 75–91; 'Biotechnologie und Ethik', *Neue Wege* 4, 1990, 103–11.

ROSEMARY RADFORD RUETHER is the Georgia Harkness Professor of Applied Theology at the Garrett-Evangelical Theological Seminary in Evanston, Illinois, USA. She is the author of numerous books and articles on feminist liberation theology, among them *Sexism and God-Talk*, Boston and London 1983; *Women-Guides: Texts for Feminist Theology*, Boston 1985; and *Women Church: Theology and Practice of Feminist Liturgical Communities*, San Francisco 1986. She has also written on Jewish-Christian relations: *Faith and Fratricide: The Theological Roots of AntiSemitism*, New York 1974; and on the religious roots of the Israeli-Palestinian conflict: *The Wrath of Jonah: The Crisis of Religious Nationalism in the Israeli-Palestinian Conflict*, San Francisco 1989.

KWOK PUI-LAN is a writer, lecturer, mother and theologian. She received her doctoral degree from Harvard University and teaches Religion and Society in the Chinese University of Hong Kong. Active in the ecumenical movement in Asia, she has lectured on Asian feminist theology in many countries in the region. She is the author of a forthcoming book, *Chinese Women and Christianity, 1860–1927*, and co-editor of *Inheriting our Mothers' Gardens: Feminist Theology in Third World Perspective*. Her articles also appear in the *East Asian Journal of Theology* and *Journal of Feminist Studies in Religion*.

MARY-JOHN MANANZAN OSB is the National Chairperson of *Gabriela*, a national federation of women's organizations in the Philippines. She is also the Dean of College of St Scholastica's College and Director of the Institute of Women's Studies. She is co-foundress of the Citizen's Alliance for Consumer Protection, of which she is the present Secretary General, and the Center for Women's Resources, of which she is the present Chairperson of the Board of Advisers.

LINDA M. MALONEY holds the PhD in American Studies from St Louis University and the ThD from the Eberhard-Karls Universität, Tübingen. She is currently Assistant Professor of New Testament Studies at the Franciscan School of Theology, Graduate Theological Union, Berkeley, California. She is the author of *All That God Had Done With Them: The Community as Described in the Acts of the Apostles*, New York 1991.

ELISABETH GÖSSMANN was born in Osnabrück in 1928. She is honorary professor at the Seishin University, Tokyo, and extra-curricular professor in the Philosophical Faculty of the University of Munich. She has written in the area of media controversy, the religious history of Japan and women's research in the history of philosophy and theology. Her works have been translated into Japanese, French, Spanish, Italian and Dutch.

SYLVIA MARCOS has researched and published on gender issues in ancient and contemporary Mexico. She was a recent recipient of the Rockefeller Humanist in Residence Award at the Women's Studies Program of Hunter College in New York City. She has been a research associate at the Women's Program for Sociology and the Psychology of Religion at Harvard Divinity School. Currently she is an international editor for *Gender and Society*, a research associate with the National Institute of Anthropology and History in Mexico, and Professor of Social Psychology at the Universidad Autonoma del Estado de Morelos. She is also a clinical psychologist in private practice in Mexico.

SARAH COAKLEY studied theology at Cambridge and Harvard. From 1976 to 1991 she was first lecturer, then senior lecturer, in Religious Studies at

Lancaster University, and is now tutorial fellow in theology at Oriel College, Oxford, where she will lecture on systematics and feminist topics. She is the author of *Christ without Absolutes*, Oxford 1988, and is currently editing a book on *Religion and the Body*, Cambridge 1991 (forthcoming). In 1982 she became the first woman to join the Church of England Doctrine Commission, and she has contributed chapters on trinitarian thought and prayer to its two most recent reports, *We Believe in God*, London 1987, and *We Believe in the Holy Spirit*, London 1991.

KATHERINE E. ZAPPONE teaches in the School of Hebrew, Biblical and Theological Studies at Trinity College, Dublin and co-directs 'The Shanty Educational Project', a programme for women and men with limited educational and economic opportunity. She edits an Irish journal on feminist spirituality, and has recently contributed an article on feminist ethics to the collection *Ethics and the Christian*, Dublin 1990. She has written *The Hope for Wholeness: A Spirituality for Feminists*, Mystic, CT 1991.

MARIA CLARA BINGEMER is married and the mother of three children. She is professor of systematic theology at the Pontifical Catholic University of Rio de Janeiro. She is a researcher at the Centro João XXIII at IBRADES in Rio de Janeiro, and Latin American regional coordinator of the Ecumenical Association of Third World Theologians (EATWOT). She gained her doctorate in theology from the Gregorian University in Rome in 1989. Her most recent publications include *O mistério de Deus na mulher*, Rio de Janeiro 1991 (edited); *O lugar da mulher*, São Paulo 1991; 'The Holy Spirit as Possibility of Universal Dialogue and Mission', in L. Swidler and P. Mohzes (ed.), *Christian Mission and Interreligious Dialogue*, Religions in Dialogue Collection, Vol. 4, Lewiston, Queeston and Lampeter 1990, 34–41; 'Solidariedade ou conflito – possibilidades de diálogo entre a Doutrina Social da Igreja e a Teologia da Libertação', *Revista Eclesiástica Brasileira* 50, 1990, 844–57.

ELIZABETH A. JOHNSON is Professor of Theology at Catholic University of America, Washington DC. She is a member of the USA Lutheran-Roman Catholic Dialogue and a past member of the Board of Directors of the Catholic Theological Society of America. She is the author of over thirty articles in theological journals, and her most recent publication is *Consider Jesus: Waves of Renewal in Christology*, New York and London 1990. Her lectures have brought her to South Africa, Canada, Mexico and numerous US universities and churches.

Members of the Advisory Committee for Feminist Theology

Directors

Anne Carr	Chicago, IL	USA
Elisabeth Schüssler Fiorenza	Cambridge, MA	USA

Members

Kari Børresen	Oslo	Norway
Bernadette Brooten	Cambridge, MA	USA
Mary Buckley	Jamaica, NY	USA
Francine Cardman	Cambridge, MA	USA
Mary Collins OSB	Washington, DC	USA
Monique Dumais	Rimouski, Quebec	Canada
Marita Estor	Bonn	West Germany
Toinette Eugene	Rochester, NY	USA
Margaret Farley	New Haven, CT	USA
Ivone Gebara	Recife	Brazil
Catharina Halkes	Nijmegen	The Netherlands
Mary Hunt	Silver Spring, MD	USA
Marianne Katoppo	Jakarta Pusat	Indonesia
Ursula King	Bristol	Great Britain
Alice Laffey	Worcester, MA	USA
Denise Lardner Carmody	Tulsa, OK	USA
Mary-John Mananzan	Manila	Philippines
Elisabeth Moltmann-Wendel	Tübingen	West Germany
Jaime Phelps OP	Washington, DC	USA
Judith Plaskow	Bronx, NY	USA
Marjorie Procter-Smith	Dallas, TX	USA
Rosemary Radford Ruether	Evanston, IL	USA
Ida Raming	Greven-Gimbte	West Germany
Christian Schaumberger	Kassel	West Germany
Sandra Schneiders IHM	Berkeley, CA	USA
Helen Schüngel-Straumann	Kassel	West Germany
Hadewych Snijdewind OP	Nijmegen	The Netherlands
Elsa Tamez	San José	Costa Rica
Beverly Wildung Harrison	New York, NY	USA

Books on Feminist Theology from SCM Press

In Memory of Her
A Feminist Theological Reconstruction of Christian Origins
Elisabeth Schüssler Fiorenza

'A serious contribution to women's history and, at the same time, it carries an argument for a major reassessment of Christian living and church structure, to the extent that they express patriarchal domination and continue to confirm it.'

(Theology)

Sexism and God Talk
Towards a Feminist Theology
Rosemary Radford Ruether

'She piles up the evidence relentlessly and it is difficult in the end not to be convinced that religious men through the ages, and still, are more keen to dominate than we admit to ourselves, and that our escape clause - the women I know are not at all oppressed - is too easy an answer.'

(New Fire)

To Change the World
Christology and Cultural Criticism
Rosemary Radford Ruether

How does belief in Christ relate to the most pressing problems of our times? By examining issues of poverty and oppression, anti- Judaism and religious intolerance, justice for the female half of the human race and the question of human survival in the face of chronic environmental abuse, this book shows that particular issues affect images of Christ as much as images of Christ affect attitudes to the issues.

Models of God
Theology for an Ecological, Nuclear Age
Sallie McFague

'It is in fact a new systematic theology, indeed a new way of thinking about systematic theology ("metaphorical theology") and materially a radically new presentation of Christian themes... It is dramatic and exciting.'

(Gordon D. Kaufman)

· **Winner of the 1988 American Academy of Religion Award for Excellence**

Books on Feminist Theology from SCM Press

Pillars of Flame
Power, Priesthood and Spiritual Maturity
Maggie Ross

'A positive affirmation and evaluation of the non-ordained of the church and a call to the ordained to reorientate themselves to the humility of Christ. The current debate needs the contribution of Maggie Ross if we are to avoid the perpetuation of power games by women as well as men.'

(Scottish Journal of Theology)

Thinking about God
Dorothee Sölle

'Here is a book which is likely to communicate the author's enthusiasm for theology - and for the practical tasks which arise out of a theologically examined and articulated faith - to people who, like herself, do not find much that excites them in more orthodox textbooks.'

(Church Times)

A time to laugh and dance...

God and the Rhetoric of Sexuality
Phyllis Trible

A new perspective on biblical language and imagery.

'Trible's brilliant rhetorical criticism, her diligent study of the Hebrew text, and her clarity about feminist hermeneutics, have indeed uncovered the lost token of faith within Scripture.'

(Sojourners)

...and a time to weep and mourn

Texts of Terror
Literary-Feminist Readings of Biblical Narratives
Phyllis Trible

'To tell and hear tales of terror is to wrestle demons in the night, without a compassionate God to save us.' A reinterpretation of the tragic stories of four women in Israel: Hagar, Tamar, an unnamed concubine and Jephthah's daughter.

Books on Feminist Theology from SCM Press

The Image and Practice of Holiness
A Critique of the Classical Manuals of Devotion
Margaret Miles

'In fact she has succeeded in fulfilling every literary critic's dream. She has written a book which sends us straight back to her primary sources by providing richly documented insights into the relevance of their imagery to our contemporary search for God.'

(Lavinia Byrne IBVM)

In Whose Image ?
God and Gender
Jann Aldredge Clanton

Ways in which the church can develop gender-inclusive images of God.

'An ironic spirit, clear writing and passionate conviction unite to make this book accessible and instructive for all who have eyes to see and ears to hear.'

(Phyllis Trible)

What Language Shall I Borrow?
Brian Wren

'What is quite simply amazing about Wren's book is that he has heard what Christian feminists say and minds about the issue. Without a trace of smirk, condescension, of doing us a favour, he struggles with his thoughts and his Christian beliefs and writes a beautiful, plangent book.'

(Monica Furlong)

All these books are available from:
SCM BOOKROOM
26-30 Tottenham Road
London N1 4BZ
Tel: 071-249 7262/5   Fax: 071-249 3776

We regret that, because of market restrictions, we are unable to supply them to customers in the US and Canada

Books on Feminist Theology from SCM Press

A Land Flowing with Milk and Honey
Elisabeth Moltmann-Wendel

'An extension into the New Testament of work already done on the Old Testament by Phyllis Trible; it is careful biblical study with a new and untraditional approach giving sharp and stimulating insights into possible interpretations of the familiar. A worthwhile book.'

(Life and Work)

God - His and Hers
Jürgen Moltmann and Elisabeth Moltmann-Wendel

Central to the Moltmanns' shared insights is the recognition that the difference between the sexes is grounded less in biology than in social experiences, so that in looking to Christian faith and practice in the future it is important to begin from the historical experience of women and men as they can be discovered from social psychology and personal testimony.

Women and Early Christianity
Are the feminist scholars right?
Susanne Heine

'Should be warmly welcome, and offers an introduction to a range of issues not readily available from other sources... Many shrewd points are made at the expense of both traditional forms of study and of feminist claims; each has too often been guilty of taking both biblical and patristic texts out of their cultural context. In this process both Paul and Tertullian receive some interesting rehabilitation.'

(King's Theological Review)

Christianity and the Goddesses
Can Christianity cope with sexuality?
Susanne Heine

'She positively urges the realization that human beings have the capacity to decide for and implement change for the better. She is one of the best representatives of a critical feminist theology demanding a *humanly* inclusive ethic.'

(Expository Times)

Issues of *Concilium* to be published in 1992

Towards the African Synod
edited by G.Alberigo and A.Ngindu Mushete

Offered as resource material in connection with the planned African Synod, and
with many African writers, this focusses on the rich historical heritage of the
African synodical tradition; surveys the situation of the churches in many
African countries, not least in the face of the challenge from Islam; examines the
African economic and political scene; traces what has so far been done (and not
done) by way of preparation for the synod.

1992/1   February

The New Europe - A Challenge for Christians
edited by N.Greinacher and N.Mette

1992 sees a major step in the development of the European community. This
issue considers the changes that it will bring and others which are needed; the
political and ethical challenges posed to Europe by the rest of the world; and the
special role of the churches in the new Europe.

1992/2   April

Fundamentalism in the World's Religions
edited by Hans Küng and Jürgen Moltmann

Begins by defining fundamentalism from both a theological and sociological
perspective; looks at the challenge of contemporary Jewish and Muslim and
Christian (Orthodox, Catholic and Protestant) fundamentalism and possible
answers to it; discusses the relationship of fundamentalism to both modernity and
postmodernity.

1992/3   June

God, Where are You? A Cry in the Night
edited by Christian Duquoc and Casiano Florestan

Studies especially the silence of God in the modern world. It examines the absence
of God in the Bible; in the experience of Jewish poets; in sickness; in the suffering
of women, the exploited and the humiliated; in distress arising from sin and in
death; and looks at the significance of this silence for church institutions.

1992/4   August

The Taboo on Democracy in the Church
edited by James Provost and Knut Walf

It is widely held that democracy is incompatible with the nature of the Catholic Church. This issue questions that assumption by examining both democracy and the nature of the church. It considers the ecclesiological implications of the theme; gives examples of democratic structures; and makes concrete proposals for the future.

1992/5   October

The Debate on Modernity
edited by Claude Geffre and Jean-Pierre Jossua

It is widely said that the modern world is now a thing of the past; we have now moved on to post-modernity. This issue looks at definitions of modernity and its relationship to Christianity; at the rise of post-modernity and criticisms of it; and at possible Christian strategies in the face of the crisis for modernity.

1992/6   December